Out of Silence

≋

Out of Silence

Emerging Themes in Asian American Churches

Fumitaka Matsuoka

United Church Press
Cleveland, Ohio

United Church Press, Cleveland, Ohio 44115

© 1995 by Fumitaka Matsuoka

Biblical quotations are from the New Revised Standard Version of the Bible, © 1989 by the Division of Christian Education of the National Council of the Churches of Christ in the U.S.A., and are used by permission

Printed in the United States of America on acid-free paper

00 99 98 97 96 95   5 4 3 2 1

Library of Congress Cataloging-in-Publication Data
Matsuoka, Fumitaka.
    Out of silence : emerging themes in Asian American churches /
Fumitaka Matsuoka.
        p. cm.
    Includes bibliographical references and index.
    ISBN 0-8298-1025-0
    1. Asian American churches. 2. Race relations—Religious
aspects—Christianity. 3. United States—Race relations. I. Title.
BR563.A7M38   1995
277.3′082′08995—dc20   94-33659
                                                              CIP

To the people of

Christ Church of Chicago

and Pastor Sharon Thornton

Contents

Preface

This work is a result of my sabbatical research on the subject of Asian American churches, the opportunity generously provided to me by Pacific School of Religion. However, my interest in this subject began during my association with and involvement in the Pacific and Asian American communities in the San Francisco Bay Area in the late 1970s and early 1980s. The wealth of "hidden" materials in the communities and the generous spirit of the Pacific and Asian American people in the Bay Area opened my eyes to the ways of human relatedness and community coherence that had not been previously available to me in this society. When I left the Bay Area and moved to Chicago, another invaluable opportunity awaited me. Christ Church of Chicago, United Church of Christ, a Japanese American congregation, welcomed my spouse and me with open arms. Eventually, my spouse was called to the congregation as its pastor and remains there in that role. My experience of the life of the congregation has provided me with a glimpse into the future of human relationships that we Christians confess in Christ. The measure of grace given to me by Christ Church of Chicago undergirds the writing of this book.

The primary issue of this book is the nature of human interactions across racial and ethnic lines in the United States.

The increasingly fragmented and alienated state of interracial and interethnic relationships is the concern that I address theologically in this work. How does Christian faith meet this serious challenge of our lives today in its incarnated form, that is, in communities of faith? Asian American churches are the context in which this issue is addressed. The experience of Asian American churches both reveals the magnitude of the fragmentation and alienation across racial and ethnic lines in the United States and offers signs of the promised humanity given to us in Christ which is the overcoming of the dividing walls of hostility that Christians confess in faith.

This work is also a modest attempt to introduce the state of Asian American Protestant churches into an ongoing discussion about contemporary American Protestantism. A dearth of materials related to Asian American churches and theology has perpetuated the "silent and invisible" status of Asian American Christians. This work is an attempt to break the silence, if a very limited attempt. A series of works by Asian American Christians intended to correct the situation are currently under way. I am confident that the silence is about to be broken.

I am grateful to the Louisville Institute of the Study of Protestantism and American Culture for providing me with a needed research grant for this work. Numerous people connected with Pacific and Asian American churches, all the way from Hawaii to California to the Midwest, have contributed to my research. Their voices represent the core of this book. Only a few names are mentioned in this work. However, I am keenly aware of the cooperation and generosity of all those whose names do not appear here but who have contributed significantly to this effort.

Finally, I would like to express my special gratitude to Greg Loving of the Graduate Theological Union for his meticulous work in editing the manuscript. Pastor Sharon Thornton of Christ Church of Chicago also played a key role in critiquing the manuscript, providing insights both from her position as pastor of a Japanese American congregation and as my loving spouse.

Introduction

Most of us are American, yet not fully acknowledged as American. Asian Americans are plagued with this awareness. We have been in the United States in significant numbers for 150 years. The first Chinese immigrant called this land *Gam Saan*, a "Gold Mountain." Asian immigrants came to this land with the promise of gold and opportunities for employment. The image of a gold mountain reflects a euphoric wish; however, the reality is that we wait years, often generations, before we become part of American society. Even then, a full acceptance into this society is not easily achieved. Today we Asian Americans find ourselves in the midst of opposing tides swirling around us. One current carries us across old enmities toward a solidarity of all people of Asian descent, another urges retreat to the nostalgia of our individual cultures and ethnic groups, and yet a third demands a just place in the larger American society, where many of us are still treated as strangers.

But we do not always live in isolation. We have vibrant communities that sustain us in our day-to-day living and give us joy in belonging to them, even in an inhospitable environment. Our Christian churches are such places of belonging. Asian American churches have remained steady and viable institutions amidst the turbulent seas of change, providing us with a sense not only of belonging, but of identity and values as well. Church gatherings, whether for worship service on Sunday morning or for an annual bazaar with the smell of teriyaki chicken wafting through the fellowship hall, have sustained a sense of community, hospitality, and acceptance for Asian Americans in an otherwise less than hospitable society. Our churches have served as a fulcrum for Asian American ethnicity.

And yet the churches are also changing, reflecting the fluid and dynamic nature of Asian American lives while attempting to accommodate the changing population. At work in all this is the power of faith to form and reform communities. Christian churches are coherent and stable institutional anchoring points for many Asian Americans. Our churches are also instrumental in helping the new generations of Asian Americans to interact with others, beyond racial and ethnic boundaries, so they may work to build a more equitable, just, and reconciled social order.

How does ethnicity inform the meaning of life for Asian Americans? What does it mean to live in the balance between two cultures or generations? How does being a minor key in the cacophony of society affect our relationship with that society? This work is an attempt to answer these questions and to understand people of Asian ancestries in the United States theologically. My first premise is that for Asian American Christians faith plays a determinative role in our attempt to respond to these questions. A good way of understanding people is to study their faith experiences.[1]

For us Christians, probing into the lives of Asian Americans is necessarily theological in character. However else theology is defined, it is at its core the attempt to make ultimacy intelligible. As such it is expressed in myriad permutations of human experiences—ethnicity, gender, culture, language, and a particular societal and historical location of people. Our theological probing centers on two points: first, how the powerful symbols of Christian faith illumine the depth of our own lives; second, how our life experiences cast a new light onto the previous articulations of faith, unmask both their limitations and potentials, and provide us with fresh articulations of faith.

My intent then is to probe the depth of the lives of Asian Americans in light of our experiences of faith, and to gain insight into our worldviews, the structures of our cosmos, and our interactions with people. Theology is perhaps an honest way of "people-understanding" for Christians. It is a refractive as well as reflective attempt to reveal the way the life of people of Asian descent is lived in this society.

Methodologically, the interiority (and therefore the subjectivity) of people of faith as they articulate the meaning of life is therefore integral to this work. Phenomenological interpretation is an appropriate tool for such an attempt. Theological articulation of the experiences of Asian American Christians calls for more than a descriptive analysis. It is necessarily both confessional and narrative in character. The experiences of participants are the foundation for theological investigation of the sacred in its incarnation in the lives of Asian Americans.

There is another motive behind this work—my second premise: it is a call to acknowledge the historical character of all theologies. It is to reveal a tendency to absolutize prior historical developments of theology and to remind ourselves of the temporal, incarnate, and often tentative character of theological endeavor. Such an acknowledgment is needed because European and European American theologies have long dominated the North American theological scene. As a consequence, they have set a standard for unhealthy power dynamics whereby the theological articulations of faith by other groups of Christians have long been relegated to the arenas of curiosity at best and trivialization at worst. What is needed is a correction of the asymmetry and a claim for the respectability of theological contributions of those whose voices have been ignored. African American, Hispanic American, American Indian, and Pacific Islander Christians have been working at this issue for some time. Some of them have begun to claim their legitimate roles in a wider theological scene in North America, and these roles have been acknowledged as such. Asian Americans have been silent. Our voices have not been heard. This book is an attempt to join the struggle of Christians of color to correct such asymmetry and disparity.

Christian faith is not available as an abstraction. The Word is made flesh in human lives. Theology is historical to its core. To phrase the issue as "Christ and culture" is to invite an absolutizing tendency (already prevalent in theological enterprise), however subtly, for it inexorably assumes the dominance of prior cultural arrangements; it easily results in making normative the particular historical propagation of some prior understanding of how Christian faith is experienced and understood by those in the position of power and influence. The real issue is how Christ lives and is experienced in a variety of particular historical settings. Theology is done *in loco et tempore*. In Asian American history, characterized by a diversity of ethnicities, cultures, spiritualities, genders, and classes, there is not likely to emerge only one theology. There is a multiplicity of theologies, with no one theology claiming dominance over the others. While this may be an obvious observation, its consequences are still disturbing to some. It is disturbing because the multiplicity of theologies delegitimizes the absolutizing of all historical developments of theology. It usurps the dominating power of the claim for the normativeness by any particular theology.

And yet the acknowledgment of the multiplicity of theologies also focuses our attention on the very incarnate character of Christian faith. It steers us away from a preoccupation with the question of universality of faith, which in itself is a peculiar cultural expression. It helps us instead to understand the depth and meaning of life more honestly and accurately even in its temporal and local characteristics. Theology is a thoroughly historical discipline that does its work in the midst of communities and their traditions. It is the discourse by which the arguments of diverse perspectives are voiced in community.

The multiplicity of theology also coincides with an alternative approach to the traditional hermeneutics which assume the normativeness and authority of the biblical texts and certain historical developments of theology. My third premise is that the primary hermeneutical approach used by Asian American Christians is to discover the questions arising out of an intersection of the saga of faith and our lives of today, and to name the theological clues out of such an interaction between the two. Such a hermeneutics eschews the uncritical collusion of a particular historical development and faith. It acknowledges a mutual interaction and interrogation between the reality claim of Christian faith and the life situation of people. Ethnicity, culture, gender, and the experiences of racism set the context for this interaction of theology and histories for Asian Americans.

Such a hermeneutical approach is properly anchored in the ecclesia, the community in which life questions and struggles of Asian Americans become focused as experience. Wallace Stevens's dictum that we do not live in a place but in a description of place applies here. By and large, theology has remained at the margins of congregational studies in the past. Many factors too complex to unravel here contribute to this marginalized status. What is needed is an articulation of the particular ecclesial theologies at work in North America. The ecclesia as experienced and described by Asian American Christians provides the setting for this theological inquiry. When Asian American churches celebrate a fall bazaar, open a senior citizens' center, or welcome people with AIDS, what motivates them? What traditions do they invoke? What beliefs and practices shape who they are and what they do? Do Scripture, sacraments, and community activities play the same roles in providing sacred encounter as they do for European Americans, or are Asian American Christians seeking new sources? How do we speak about the transcendent, the sacred, God? What do our religious architecture, music, and art tell us about our sense of the sacred? What rituals are spiritually salient? How do people's private spiritual quests intersect with the piety we experience in our churches?

Something more is needed here than simply applying denominational, ecumenical, or historical theologies to the particular ecclesial setting. We need to discover how communities of faith shape their own theologies, weaving together strands from cultures, ethnicities, histories, spiritualities, personal experiences, and whatever else seeps into the faith community from a pluralistic environment. My fourth premise is that Christianity is primarily a matter of practice within a particular historical setting and that it is in practice that the key theological issues are found. I use the term "practice" to mean cooperative human activities that are socially established over time.[2] Communal life is constituted by practices. Too often, however, we think of community as a group of people who share a common history and a set of well-defined beliefs and visions. While this is partially true, a community's diversity and disagreements are also real. They are signs of both vibrancy and life of a community. It is also here that the most difficult complications and contradictions arise theologically, creating opportunities for a contrary truth to emerge.

Methodologically, what I propose is to let theological issues and questions emerge from the voices of the Asian American people in the church. The task is phenomenological in character. It is to make as precise as possible the shape of the experience being investigated. This approach takes into account the complex web of interrelated signs, symbols, and actions, or what Clifford Geertz has called the "thick description" of the congregation. Theological questions are detected through the discovery of the patterns inherent in the "multiplicity of complex conceptual structures, many of [which] are superimposed upon or knotted into one another, which are at once strange, irregular, and inexplicit."[3] By utilizing what E. H. Schein calls "properties" within a given culture—artifacts, perspectives, strategic values, and assumptions—some intelligible contour of the ecclesia can be discerned.[4]

A word of caution is in order. A theological reflection done in an ethnographic and phenomenological fashion offers the author the opportunity to re-encounter the church "safely," to find meaning in the chaos of limited experience through retrospectively ordering the observation. It is a kind of Proustian quest in which the author seeks meaning in events whose significance is elusive while they are being lived. We are reminded of the words of Eva Hoffman in *Lost in Translation*: "It is no wonder, in our time of mass migrations and culture collisions and easy jet travel, . . . that we have devised a whole metaphysics for the subjects of difference and otherness. But for all our sophisticated deftness at cross-cultural encounters, fundamental difference, when it's staring at you across the table from within the close-up face of a fellow human being, always contains an element of violation." If the primary task of this writing is to produce theological reflection that articulates accurately the experiences of Asian American churches, it is crucial that we allow for these churches to defy the previously held understandings of churches, to allow their different ways of making sense to "take over" the research project. Staying close to Asian American churches' conceptual categories and reflecting on their voices that are central to this writing, I hope I've allowed for enough creative "misbehavior" to emerge. Admittedly, I have found myself deeply enmeshed in the subject of this research, Asian American churches. Objectivity in the research has not been possible. My personal participation in the "internal history" of Asian American churches is integral to their theological discernment.

Theological thinking in such a setting is temporal in character. Such a theology sees temporality as a crucial dimension of faith as a living, developing phenomenon and accepts the ethnically and culturally conditioned character of all human knowledge as a sign that the transcendent God has become incarnate in human history and culture.

The fifth premise I bring to this work is that Christian faith that transcends all histories is stated communally in terms of each particular history. To say this is to recognize the mosaic and unfolding character of Christian faith. It is also a reminder that faith understanding is communal and collaborative in character and is not to be undertaken in isolation. Theology has mostly been the work of lone individuals. Only recently have collegial and collaborative attempts begun, mainly among women and racially and ethnically underrepresented groups of Christians. Even here the mere proclamation of faith by one group of people, ethnic or otherwise, denies the integrity, the reality, and the potential of other groups.

Theological enterprise in North America needs not only to exhibit caution against the absolutizing of the theology of a particular group, especially that of the dominant group. Churches need also to seek the redemption of a new tomorrow, one in which, through the unique composite and the voice of community, members can claim their rightful place as God's children. The liberation of each group shall be the bond that unites us all. This is the conviction which undergirds this work. The question to be posed is this: How do communally voiced Christian faith experiences of Asian Americans speak to the ways we affirm the common symbols and to a coherence with various other ethnic and cultural groups in this society, while retaining the awareness their our own distinctness?

This work is admittedly preliminary in nature with an eye toward a more comprehensive attempt to understand Asian American churches in the future. Such an attempt will most likely be done collectively, with the participation of a wider group of people. This study is limited to four ethnic churches of mainline Protestantism: Christians of Chinese, Filipino, Japanese, and Korean ancestries. Their voices are collected among four geographical regions: the Chicago area, Hawaii, the San Francisco Bay Area, and the Los Angeles area.

The research method employed for this work consists of ethnographic survey, historical research, and interviews. It is an approach that assumes that every community of faith has its own distinctive pattern of meaning and method of articulating it. My primary intent is to understand the behaviors, customs, interactions, social networks, feelings, and artifacts of the communities of faith from inside and to determine what these signify to its members. I looked for patterns in the interviews and conversations that would yield a list of themes that dominate the Asian American churches' behavioral activities. These themes provided a theological interpretation of what is distinctive in the subculture of the community of faith. I should also note that my participation in the internal history of Asian American churches provides a particular angle of vision to this project. To a significant extent, this work reflects my own personal journey of faith, which is juxtaposed with the communal journey of Asian American Christians.

A crucial issue in the research was the split in Asian American churches between those who are satisfied with the structural "corporate" church and those who seek a more demanding "spiritual" communitas.[5] These differences can be seen (1) in their attitudes toward the larger society, (2) in their orientation toward communal organization, and (3) in their expectations of pastoral leadership. The question regarding this issue was posed in order to examine the place of Asian Americans relative to other groups in society. Are we indeed "strangers from a different shore" in America, as Ronald Takaki observes in his book of that title?[6] How do our experiences within a particular social and historical location affect our faith experiences, and vice versa?

In this work I will also explore the pattern of symbols by which a particular community of faith gives meaning to its life and language. Literary symbolism works with these same components—pattern, meaning, and language—to reveal how human imagination gives narrative structure to corporate life.[7] In describing anthropology, Clifford Geertz talks of its uncovering what Max Weber termed a society's "webs of significance." There are patterns of shared beliefs and values that give the members of an institution meaning, and provide them with the rules for behavior in their organization. There are also shared philosophies, ideologies, values, assumptions, beliefs, expectations, attitudes, and norms that knit a community together. In combining ethnography and literary criticism I am most concerned with finding the webs of meaning that shape the culture of Asian American people.

I have also paid special attention to the narrative historical accounts that are often the source of these cultural themes. The act of recounting one's life journey, collectively or individually, is an important means of understanding an intersection between faith and life. When a survey was done among the constituents of twenty-five Japanese American Christian churches in 1982, it was noted that the types of books they enjoyed reading the most (40 percent) were biographies—i.e., true stories about people, particularly their own stories.[8] "With integrity and authenticity, we must look within ourselves for the stories. With compassion and grace we must look within the lives of our people for their stories. And with wisdom and objectivity, we must peer at the events of this world—especially the incarnation, death, and resurrection of Jesus—for the chapters in God's kingdom-story," writes Kenneth Uyeda-Fong.[9]

Christianity is one of the majority religions among Asian Americans, even though it is a minority religion in many of the countries from which we and our ancestors came. This fact signals the significance of Christian churches in our lives. Like all immigrants and refugees before us, we Asian Americans inexorably find ourselves on a common road to assimilation. And yet our "racial uniform" makes it difficult to gain acceptance in the larger society. We are often "judged not by the content of our character but by our complexion."[10]

Asian American churches are one of the few institutions in which that is not the case. We have found acceptance, respectability, and relationships in our communities of faith. The churches have served as the locus not only of fostering our spirituality but also of cultivating our sense of belonging in an otherwise less than hospitable environment.

And yet our churches are also the institutions that isolate us from the wider world by race and ethnicity. They are bearers of an ambiguous self-image for Asian Americans. My thesis is that these ambiguous and sometimes contradictory postures of the Asian American Protestant communities mirror the dynamic and changing scene of our ethnicity from which a new and different Asian American culture is being forged. Our churches are one of the primary settings for the emergence of this new culture that transcends the previously held perceptions of human groupings. The various expressions of our heightened ethnic assertiveness; our experiences of cultural, generational, and spiritual liminality; and the ever-present reminders of human propensity toward sin in the form of racism we encounter—all are proleptic signs of what this new Asian American culture may evolve toward.

Asian American churches are *ecclesia semper reformanda* (a church forming and reforming), being open to new and ever-greater exploration. Can our churches become communities that enable Asian Americans to interact with other groups to chart the course of society and culture for a reconciled and just social order? Our life together in our churches, both its pain and promise, is deeply theological in character. In our churches our religious faith and our daily lives intersect with each other. And in our churches we see a glimpse of the path Asian Americans will walk in this ever-changing culture. This book is a modest attempt to discern the symbols and signals of the world of Asian American Christians as we gather in our communities of faith.

≋ 1

Christian Faith
and Asian American Ethnicity
A Quest to Meet the Longing of Our Heart

*With the increasing trend towards multi-culturalism, the Korean
Church may seem like an elitist bastion. At the same time, I
think the church is dynamic, trying to accommodate the changing
Korean population, both immigrants and second and third gener-
ation Koreans. I go to a small East Coast school with a lot of
very different kinds of people, so it's kind of nice to have a
Korean-American church nearby to go to and feel a part of
Korean culture."* [1]

The survival and flourishing of an ethnic group in our society
depends largely upon the vitality of its center. If that vitality
cannot be sustained, pluralism will prove to be a temporary phenomenon, a way station on the road to acculturation. Historically, churches have played an anchoring role in ethnicity for
many immigrant Americans. Ethnicity, says Martin Marty, is "the
skeleton of religion in America because it provides 'the support-
ing framework,' 'the bare outlines or main features,' of American
religion." [2] For African Americans, claim Eric Lincoln and
Lawrence Mamiya, black churches are indeed "the key to understanding this entire subculture," these churches having served as

the only stable and coherent institutional area to emerge from slavery with its own distinctness.[3] For Asian Americans, too, churches have served as the locus of ethnic vitality for a large number of people. They are by no means the "white church" with Asian faces. The church is a center that has held together our ethnicities. The church also provides both a framework of meaning that explains the events of our lives and a sense of belonging and identity in an often inhospitable society. The church is an important source of our moral authority in the confusion of values and mores swirling around us. For Asian American Christians the church is the place of our quest to meet the longing of our hearts. In our quest we are met by nothing less than the grace of the One who restores us to our authentic human selves. The church has served as a primary locus for the emergence of distinct Asian American cultures in our society. The relationship of ethnicity and faith as reflected in the communal life of Asian American churches is therefore a significant arena of theological inquiry How is the sense of communal self experienced and understood in the development of Asian American churches?

Historically, many Asian immigrants relied upon Christian churches to sustain them in the new and often harsh environment of North America. Korean American churches, for instance, were a center of the Korean American community as the independence movement from Japanese occupation united the initial wave of Korean immigrants prior to World War II. Today churches continue to serve as a significant locus of Korea American community life. Japanese and Chinese American Christian churches have helped those groups to retain their cultural heritage and ethnic coherence, which are fast eroding in an era when "out-marriage"—marrying across ethnic and racial lines—is commonplace. "Many of us have come to see in congregations a quasi-housing authority, makeshift employment office, supplementary educational system, recreation and park agency, and communication network—to say nothing of the potential religious dimension that the caring community provides," recalls Bishop Roy Sano of the United Methodist Church.[4] Filipino American churches represent a blending of three waves of immigration spanning nearly ninety years. Their churches are a remarkable reflection of subgroupings that have developed over linguistic, regional, and class differences. Filipino American churches serve as a cohering center of these differences among people. "Churches through our education have helped Filipino laborers recover a sense of pride in our history and heritage without which they cannot survive here, particularly in plantations," says Patria Augustin, a Filipino pastor in Honolulu.

And yet there has been a subtle but gradual shift taking place in recent years among Asian American churches. Ethnicity is no longer just survival for Asian American Christians. Maxine Hong Kingston, a novelist and educator, argues that Asian American ethnicity is now the issue of claiming our rightful place in American history and in society.[5] The very existence of our churches means that we are not invisible in this society. Just as our humanity is affirmed within our churches, Asian American churches call for an acknowledgment of our rightful place in the wider society as legitimate members. What do these signs of change in our churches indicate? What are the "glues" that hold us together in the community of faith? These are the questions that will be posed in this chapter.

Contradictory Postures in the Era of Manifest Destiny

A composite picture will show that Asian American churches have historically held two contradictory and ambiguous postures in regard to their places in U.S. society. On the one hand, they have played a critical role in building and sustaining community for their own peoples. In the church, people found a place to gather, to see familiar faces, and to partake of a familiar culture. Many church activities were Western in form, but were indigenized in content. To be sure, churches also functioned to transmute culture. Asian activities were blended with Western church practices and some traditions were given Christian meaning. Churches also provided or secured needed social services for the community. All in all, it can be said that there was no area of community need that the church did not at one time or another address.

On the other hand, as carriers of a particular American religious and cultural tradition inherited from Europe, Asian American churches often served to set that tradition against Asian American communities. The style of organization and operation of these churches was informed by social and cultural values of the European American dominant group and often became confounded with its religious values. Pastor J. W. Smith of Koloa, Kauai, calling for more mission work to be done among the Chinese immigrants, wrote in 1879:

> It seems to me to be the highest wisdom to make all possible effort to Christianize the Chinese amongst us. Here they are at our doors, and here they will stay; and their number will increase; and they will be either heathen or Christian. The people of California would have done better to have made a grand effort to evangelize the Chinese instead of the futile effort to drive them out of the country. Let us profit by their mistake.[6]

To become Christian, to a certain extent, was to become American. To be American was to become Christian. This was true particularly in the early days of the Asian immigration to the U.S. In this interplay it was assumed that civilization was best reflected in a Christian America. Asian Americans then viewed the churches as a major route and catalyst towards assimilation. But assimilation really meant accommodation into the values of the dominant cultural group. Many Asian customs and activities were criticized as uncivilized or pagan in the Asian American churches. The only element that seemed legitimate was language, but even here the native Asian languages were used to carry translated prayers, hymns, and liturgies. William Shinto, a Japanese American pastor, noticed that many children of Buddhist families enrolled in the church school of the congregation that he served in Los Angeles. "I believe that many did this so that their children could learn about Christianity, the religion of the West, in hope of mitigating White racism."[7] Buddhism, unlike Christian churches, had to "fight the image of being a foreign faith. Although the hostility to the religion itself is now tempered, this was not always the case. For example, at the beginning of World War II, Buddhist priests in America were jailed as enemy agents. In fact, one of the key issues still to be resolved is the public recognition that Buddhists are indeed American and their faith is not alien."[8]

Christian churches by and large did not carry such a cultural stigma. When Chinese churches were established in San Francisco and Sacramento in the 1850s, America was a Protestant culture, a European American Protestant culture. It was the "only national religion and to ignore that fact is to view the country from a false angle," said Andre Siegfried.[9] Protestant churches of the day epitomized this basic worldview. To be sure, not everybody practiced religion at the birth of this nation. But those elite who did were Protestant, and they were the "norm-givers" and "name-givers" in early America. "One people, one state," the maxim of John Jay, captures a long tradition of thought that began at the birth of this nation. The Americans "descended from the same ancestors, speaking the same language, professing the same religion, attached to the same principles of government, very similar in their manners and customs." They "should never be split into a number of unsocial, jealous, and alien sovereignties."[10] Jay's words are indicative of the basic worldview behind the ethos of the European American Protestant leadership regarding the U.S. society at its early stage of history. Their goal was the homogeneity of all people. This meant that the very cohesiveness of American society depended upon the assimilation of diverse groups of people into this particular idea of homogeneity developed by the particular cultural and ethnic group occupying the dominant role in society. This worldview carries the weight of European history, particularly the political ideal nurtured by the Christian empire of the Middle Ages. One religious communion, it was argued, made one political community. The religiously mixed empires of ancient and modern times, by contrast, had few theoretical defenders, only publicists and apologists.

Andre Siegfried noted that America had developed as an

essentially Calvinistic country where a Reformed perspective nurtured "the feeling of social obligation that is so typically Anglo-Saxon." This feeling is responsible for "the missionary spirit which animates the crusades against cigarettes, alcohol, and the slums, and such movements as feminism, pacifism, anti-vivisection, Americanization of immigrants, and even the gospel of eugenics and birth control."[11] This residual Calvinism, though broadened into a mostly secular creed, explains why "every American is at heart an evangelist, be he a Wilson, a Bryan, or a Rockefeller," and why "he cannot leave people alone, and . . . constantly feels the urge to preach."[12]

This residual Calvinism was formative in the notion of one people making one state. The underlying political philosophy of the authors of *The Federalist Papers* (1787–88) reflected this long tradition of thought. In enacting the Naturalization Law of 1790, the First Congress of the United States affirmed its commitment to the "pure principles of Republicanism" and its determination to develop a citizenry of good and "useful men," a homogeneous society.[13] As immigrants from various cultural, religious, and national backgrounds began to arrive in the mid-nineteenth century, "one people, one state" was no longer reflective of the reality. The society was composed of many peoples, sharing residence and in some cases citizenship only, without a common cultural history. Politically, cohesion was needed. Culturally, however, homogeneity remained intact. While the slogan *e pluribus unum* ("from many, one") eventually became the political foundation of American society, the operative worldview remained the same: the immigrants would one day constitute a single people.

Korean American Christian Philip Park described this underlying worldview behind the establishment of late-nineteenth-century Asian American churches: "Asian American history and Asian American church history cannot really be separated."[14] Protestant home mission boards saw the Asian immigrants as objects of missionary zeal, people to be "converted" and immigrants to be assimilated into one America. Such "conversion" took place in the backdrop of American expansion into Asia, or what Admiral Alfred Thayer Mahan called "Race Patriotism." "Considering the American states as members of the European family, as they are by traditions, institutions, and languages, it is in the Pacific, where the westward course of empire again meets the East, that their relations to the future of the world become most apparent."[15] Sydney Ahlstrom attributes this posture to American Protestantism's "strong reassertion of God's absolute sovereignty in all that pertained to the natural order and to the salvation of his people."[16] Churches for Asian immigrants were established within this cultural, religious, and political context of the mid-nineteenth century. "One people, one state" gave direction and force to the establishment of Protestant churches for Asian new arrivals in the era of Manifest Destiny.

When the Presbyterian Board of Foreign Missions began its first Chinese Mission in 1852, the initial purpose was to attend to the sick and poorly fed who came to *Gam Saan* ("Gold Mountain") from China aboard old and rotting ships: "Regular preaching in their own language was commenced during the winter, which was well attended. A church was organized on November 6th, 1853, composed of several men who had been members in China. This was the first Chinese church in the New World."[17] The church soon opened "a night school, with which was connected lectures on astronomy, geography, chemistry and other sciences, illustrated by proper apparatus or a magic lantern."[18] A gradual process of accommodation into the dominant culture of that time had begun.

Other Chinese missions sponsored by different denominations followed in the same period—the Baptist Church of Sacramento in 1854, the Episcopal Church in San Francisco between 1855 and 1856, and the Methodist Episcopal Church in San Francisco in 1868. All these were run by European American missionaries who had previously worked in China. The Protestant European American churches at that time equated the fear of divisiveness, turmoil, and repression with the cultural and social isolation of the Chinese from the predominant European American worldview. Chinese American churches served as a catalyst to counter such a tendency and to facilitate the assimilation of Chinese into the prevailing social and national conscious-ness of "from many, one." Pastor Gilbert Lum lamented as late as 1958, "Christianity as practiced here is too often a brand of American Christianity which is mainly to preserve the 'Ameri-can Way of Life.'"[19]

Jose Movido, a Filipino clergy person in the Los Angeles area, observed that Filipino Methodist churches, which origi-nated before World War II as distinct ethnic churches, gradually desegregated when they were absorbed into the new structure of Annual Conferences and jurisdictions as mandated by General Conferences.[20] "While Methodist churches in the Los Angeles area affirmed the presence of Filipinos among them, they were simply names on the church roll, and few of them were ad-mitted into the inner circles of administrative councils," recalls Artemio R. Guillermo, president of the National Filipino Ameri-can United Methodists.[21]

Americanization was aimed at peoples susceptible to cul-tural change. Some denominational home mission agencies be-came an instrument for assimilation of Asian Americans under the pretense of imparting a "moral" influence on those who were living in an unstable frontier society. This was particularly the case for early Japanese immigrants. Japanese churches were estab-lished in the late nineteenth century for the isseis, the immigrant Japanese, to meet the need for companionship and mutual sup-port while living in an often hostile and alien society. "The church stood firm against gambling, prostitution, and liquor. . . . The church preached to maintain the sacredness of homelife and social justice, protecting escaped prostitutes. Prohibition of smoking and drinking were practiced in the church family, which . . . were a hindrance to newcomers and the public in joining the church."[22] The inner-worldly asceticism of Protestantism was vividly present in the initial stage of the history of Japanese American churches, leaving its significant imprint upon the shape of the churches to come.

The first Japanese Christian group to form was composed of eight students who in 1877 organized *Fukuin Kai* (the Gospel Fellowship Circle) in San Francisco. "By the warm and enthusiastic assistance of White American Church members they met to learn English and study the Bible."[23] Gradually, networks of Protestant churches were established throughout the United States and Canada by various denominational groups. The need for a cultural haven was one of the reasons for church establishment. Japanese Americans could continue their cultural practices, such as celebrating Japanese holidays, in churches. Churches also provided or secured needed social services for the community.

At the same time, many viewed churches as a major route and catalyst towards assimilation, which in reality meant accommodation to the values of the dominant European American social order. Early Asian immigrants found membership in Christian churches as a way to be quickly identified as American and avoid being continually labeled "alien." Some immigrants assumed that one quick, acceptable way to assimilate was to convert to Christianity, the principal faith and major cultural force of the land. Youth groups and then women's fellowships were organized in which "mothers would get together to discuss the education of the children and the mother's role in the family. Many mothers joined the church through such hopes, and the Christian way of life that attracted them."[24] Today many churches continue to offer programs to meet the needs of new arrivals. Eleanor Mercado, one of only a handful of Filipino North American models in Chicago, realized early that language is probably the greatest obstacle to assimilation. Just a week after she moved into her new home from the Philippines, a new school year started. "It was hard because I didn't know how to speak English," she says. Today when Mercado's parents speak to her at home in their native language, she answers in English. "It's not bad to keep your culture," she says, "but you should try to blend in." The loss of language means the loss of cultural and spiritual values carried over from Asia. Christian churches have assisted Asian Americans in their acquisition of English language skills and as a result have contributed to the erosion of their Asian identities. Hard-core ethnicity seldom survives a second generation in this society under such circumstances.

"From many, one," with its underlying worldview of the cultural hegemony, took on a curious but disturbing twist at the outbreak of World War II for Japanese Americans: the incarceration of all persons of Japanese ancestry. While war hysteria and racial prejudice played a major role in the Roosevelt administration's decision in favor of the internment, an equally important factor was the administration's desire to assimilate the culturally isolated ethnic group of Japanese and Japanese Americans, argues Richard Drinnon in *Keeper of the Concentration Camps*.[25] Through a compilation of memoranda, quotations, writings, and policies, Drinnon demonstrates that those who led the War Relocation Authority (WRA) were a "walking repository of the Puritan virtues and traditional hostility to the very idea of the survival of separate peoples with separate cultures."[26] Both Japanese and Japanese Americans were to be treated as "mysteries to be solved, inscrutable Orientals, perils to be guarded against, abstractions, symbols, all subsumed under the epithet 'Japs.'"[27] In order to be moved from the West Coast, they were told either to enter "Relocation" centers or to migrate to the east. Clearly the WRA intended by "relocation" to fully assimilate the Japanese Americans by eliminating the "Little Tokyo" cultural centers and dispersing the members of this culture throughout the whole nation, where they would be in constant contact with the dominant American culture. Together the Japanese constituted the "yellow peril"; separated, they were individual groupings forced to adapt to the dominant social and cultural order in order to survive. "You had virtual cultural genocide, fifty years of assimilation crammed into less than one decade," says Ruth Sasaki, author of *The Loom and Other Stories*.[28]

While the tragic event of mass evacuation was not widely known by the bulk of Americans, some Christians and Jews responded to the plight of Japanese Americans by establishing the Japanese American Student Relocation Council, headquartered in Philadelphia. Denominations such as the American Friends Service and the Church of the Brethren also assisted in the relocation of Japanese Americans to the Chicago area. In retrospect, despite good intentions and with deep gratitude expressed by those who benefited from the relocation efforts, the churches that helped relocate Japanese Americans inadvertently contributed to their assimilation into the dominant culture.

The American ideal of cultural homogeneity, "from many, one," exerted its power over Japanese Americans in one of the most vulnerable periods of their history. The fear of divisiveness, and also simply of difference, drove U.S. society to extremes in protecting the cultural hegemony expressed in the constitutional ideal. Many of those interned in the camps were U.S.-born citizens. Now they were to be naturalized again, not politically but culturally. *E pluribus unum* took a dark turn in its expression. American Protestant churches were by and large uncritical of this acculturation of Japanese Americans.

However, this tenacious power of homogenization was met equally by the tenacity of the Japanese American community to protect its ethnic integrity. While the process of assimilation was not totally opposed by citizens of Japanese descent even in the midst of their painful experiences of incarceration, the preservation and legitimization of their own community was paramount in their mind. Such an attempt took on a strange, painful, and seemingly contradictory expression in Japanese Americans' posture toward the U.S. government during their internment.

While the administration and the WRA pushed its goal of ethnic and cultural dispersion, some Japanese American Christian leaders even began to contend that "under the circumstances, it probably was the wisest thing for the government to do."[29] Some pastors in internment called for the internees to enlist in the U.S. armed forces. A letter written by a Japanese pastor in one of the internment camps reveals this sentiment:

> *Dear Nobuo, You have dedicated yourself to your country. It is a beautiful thing. I am proud of you. . . . I am sure through your own dedication you can understand the great meaning of the sacrifice of Jesus Christ on the cross. He dedicated himself to the kingdom of God just as you have dedicated yourself to the beautiful America that you hold in your*

heart. Jesus Christ fought a good fight, and when the time came, he sacrificed himself on his battle front, the cross.

I want you to fight bravely for your nation and for humanity, and if it is necessary, sacrifice yourself for your nation just as Jesus Christ did on the cross for the Kingdom of God.[30]

Such religious sentiment was not alien to the Japanese American Christians who experienced internment. Koji Murata recalls a Sunday service at Topaz Relocation Camp. The pastor urged the congregation: "Instead of cursing the darkness, let's brighten the room with candlelights like stars in the sky." "I thought that was wonderful that stars shine in the darkness of the sky, . . . that we be the light bearers."[31] Lester Suzuki of the United Methodist Church observes that "the situation with watch towers with guns, and the open worship services where anyone could come, did not allow for the most prophetic preaching."[32] While the ministries in the camps were more pastoral than prophetic, the sacrificial spirit of Japanese Americans was dramatically emblazoned, in the public's view, by the ultimate sacrifice of the celebrated all-nisei (second-generation) "suicide" 442nd Regiment and the 100th Battalion. Undoubtedly these sacrificial acts had some effect in tempering the extreme form of war hysteria in society at large. However, the question still lingers: Why did Japanese Americans who were interned unjustly and unconstitutionally behind the barbed-wire fences of Manzanar, Poston, Minidoka, and other War Relocation Center camps volunteer to serve in the war theaters of Europe and the Pacific so willingly?

Karty Fujita, a native of the East Coast, echoes this puzzlement of many younger generation Japanese Americans: "it bothered me, like the 442nd, for example, if I felt they were doing it for this country, for America first and foremost as good loyal Americans and it was the main reason, that wouldn't sit well. That would bother me and it would always be there."[33]

A glimpse into this puzzle comes from a letter to a young Japanese woman in Hawaii written by one of the nisei soldiers:

> By virtue of the Japanese attack on our nation, we as Ameri-
> can citizens of Japanese ancestry have been mercilessly flogged
> with criticism and accusations. But I'm not going to take it
> sitting down! I may not be able to come back. But that mat-
> ters little. My family and friends—they are the ones who will
> be able to back their arguments with facts. They are the ones
> who will be proud. In fact, it is better that we are sent to the
> front and that a few of us do not return, for the testimony will
> be stronger in favor of the folks back home.[34]

Karty Fujita reflects: "But if I hear, maybe they're doing it for their own people, then it has a lot of meaning to me. . . ."[35] In the face of the powerful force toward assimilation, even in its extreme form of incarceration into concentration camps, a ethnic genocide, a counter force to preserve the dignity of their ethnic community and its coherence was equally present among them.

But the price Japanese Americans have paid for the preser-vation of their dignity is both extremely painful and immeasur-able, passed on to succeeding generations. Some sanseis (third generation) have begun to discover that their experiences of emotional, psychological, and spiritual conflict and cultural dis-comfort have significant roots in the internment camps—or more precisely, in the ways their nisei parents reacted to the internment camps. Furthermore, the sanseis' growing under-standing of the camp experience serves as a window into both the pre–World War II years and the family and community expe-riences that have had an impact on their lives today. This issue will be treated more extensively in chapter 2.

A durable sense of ethnicity, or "peoplehood," as Martin Marty calls it, is a critical factor in understanding the larger American community. This is also the case for Asian American communities. The tenacity of Asian American ethnic con-sciousness is expressed in Asian American churches, which are a cultural haven amid the turbulent sea of American society. In these churches, newly arrived Asian immigrants could continue their cultural practices, such as celebrating the holidays of the native lands. The churches have also served as a buffer against the onslaught of European American cultural forces. "Ethnicity in American historiography has remained something of a family scandal, to be kept a dark secret or explained away," says Rudolph J. Vecoli.[36] And yet churches have tenaciously maintained the strength and vitality of Asian American ethnicity even while the European American Protestant community exerts its powerful influence upon the whole society. In mid-century, European American Protestantism lost power as a result of the displacement of Protestant majorities by non-Protestant immigrants and those from other religious and ethnic traditions. Asian American churches have also contributed to this disestablishment of the Protestant cultural hegemony. They have done so by accentuating a view of society as consisting of subcultures, or a "nation of nationalities," as Horace Kallen called it.

But the emergence of a pluralistic society in the United States is met by tremendous resistance, as the history of African American subculture suggests. The forces of assimilation work to undermine the communal confidence of ethnic enclaves. The counterforce against assimilation calls for energy, enthusiasm, and commitment within each subculture.

Asian American churches have coped with these challenges in numerous ways. One such way is to "choose" the cultural tradition to which one was born. Michael Yoshii, pastor of Buena Vista United Methodist Church in Alameda, California, traces the origin of the annual church bazaar to the Doll Festival (*Hinamatsuri*), which is carried over from the Japanese cultural tradition. The dolls decorated for the church bazaar "are reminders that culture is not static, but is always changing. And although these dolls are rooted in stories and meaning created out of ancient Japan, their meaning can be transformed when we see them as living culture, as witnesses to a living and dynamic history."[37] In her book *Desert Exile*, Yoshiko Uchida describes how her mother regularly observed certain Japanese customs and took great pains to display dolls for Doll Festival Day. After her mother's death, Yoshiko carries on the tradition, but for new

reasons: "it is not so much in remembrance of Doll Fe
that I display them [the dolls] as in remembrance of r
and her Japanese ways."[38] An act of remembering leads to the
transformation of traditional Asian culture into new expressions
of Asian American culture and thus becomes part of the legacy of
new generations.

In Hawaii, English language classes and the fostering of the
European American values by early missionaries accelerated the
process of assimilation for Chinese Christians. While this was
going on, "Chinese culture was not altogether forsaken and, in
fact, was clearly evident in early church architecture and interior
design, in the ever-prevalent Chinese food, and in societal proto-
col that included respect for elders and scholar-priests. The very
use of the Chinese language in worship services was a way of
retaining a cultural handle on Christianity."[39]

Ethnic awareness is particularly strong among Korean American churches. The early immigrants were quick to organize Christian churches. Soon after their arrival they started churches in
Honolulu (1903), then in Los Angeles (1904), the San Francisco
Bay Area, southern California, New York, and Chicago. Most of
the early immigrants in Hawaii eventually became involved with
these churches, which became the centers of social, educational,
and community affairs. Korean American churches perpetuated
the traditional values of Korea. Church schools taught the immigrants and their children to read and speak Korean, wiping out
illiteracy by 1915. The schools also taught Korean songs and
dances to the younger generation, and published newspapers and
magazines. Korean American churches perpetuated the traditional values of Korea. The ministers who served as interpreters
and social workers became intermediaries between the immigrants
and American society. Equally important, the churches were centers of the Korean national independence movement, the principal thread unifying the community prior to 1945. Today Christian
churches are still an important cohering power among the Korean
American population. "Christian churches are the most important social and cultural institutions for Koreans in America,"
proclaims Eui-Young Yu, professor of sociology at California State

University, Los Angeles.[40] Nearly 70 percent of the Koreans in America are affiliated with the church. Korean American churches are indeed powerful focal points of social, cultural, and ethnic interaction for the majority of the immigrants and serve as the center of their community life. "Through church meetings they make friends and exchange information on jobs, business, social service benefits, children's schooling, and so on."[41] It is noteworthy, however, that very few churches have adequate programs in English. "The first generation dominated churches have yet to establish a system of meaningful dialogue with English speaking Korean children," laments Eui-Young Yu.[42] The vitality of Korean American ethnicity is nevertheless clearly embodied in their churches.

Not all the church experiences of Asian Americans are positive, however. "We've been inundated by our parents all our lives: Keep your history, keep your language, keep your culture," says Sang Shim, a twenty-one-year-old student at the University of Illinois. "I grew up attending a Korean church. We have a Korean household. I feel lost out on American friends and culture. I play on the [men's] volleyball team at school, and I feel there is a distance between myself and the white players." Nevertheless, many younger-generation Korean American Christians affirm the role their churches play in their lives. John G. Ha, of Northbrook, Illinois, a nineteen-year-old sophomore at Dartmouth College, observes, "With the increasing trend towards multiculturalism, the Korean church may seem like an elitist bastion. At the same time, I think the church is dynamic, trying to accommodate the changing Korean population, both immigrants and second- and third-generation Koreans."

To survive, many Asian immigrants have drawn upon elements of their culture—family and community relationships, language, religion, values, traditions, recreation, art—to sustain them. "Community of Memory" is the way Ronald Takaki describes Asian Americans' claim for their ethnicity.[43] "As they listen to the stories and become members of a 'community of memory,' they are recovering roots deep within this country and the homelands of their ancestors."[44] In the face of poverty, racially motivated violence, inadequate housing, alienation, and strains on family life, Christian churches have been the "community of memory" for many Asian Americans. Sharon Thornton, pastor of Christ Church of Chicago, United Church of Christ, a Japanese American congregation, says:

> No one has to tell us who we are or where we belong, or what values are important to us. Specific instructions are not always given on all this. No one has to explain that sense of belonging and appreciation. We learn about it though, through participating in the community. It is through events like Akimatsuri (Fall Bazaar) that we are initiated, nurtured, and claimed into this family we call church. It is here that we participate in common memories and stories.[45]

The "community of memory" unites the joy and the sorrow, the caring and callousness, the promise and broken promise. It shapes and defines the being of Asian Americans and creates cultural structures for our expression. The community is unifying because it affirms that our own peoplehood is possible only in a communal context. It is the affirmation of a common bond for those who are otherwise threatened with dispersion into the wider, amorphous, and often hostile environment.

It is practically impossible to talk about Christian faith without acknowledging the deep spirituality that has been nurtured by our memories of the past, both ethnically and culturally. "[I]f I worship the dead, it is because I hear my parents whispering through the marrow of my bones asking to be fed," writes Nellie Wong.[46] Christian faith is incarnational to its core. In our participation in particular "communities of memory," with their cultural, ethnic, and spiritual peculiarities, we see the principal place of a Christian identity, sustenance, conversion, and growth. Our experiences as Asian Americans and our expressions of those experiences may be unfamiliar to our European American Christian tradition. The dynamic relationship between faith and ethnicity expressed within Asian American churches may appear to include some syncretistic amalgamation of cultures and spiritualities we inherited from Asia into what has been considered "normative" for Christian faith. What is theologically at stake, however, is the recognition of the one living God incarnate in the life of all peoples. Just as European Christians did as they built their tradition from before Nicaea and Chalcedon, Asian Americans are doing by forging expressions of faith within our own ethnic, cultural, and historical context. This calls for a much larger view of Christian faith than the ones developed in the past. It challenges us to consider what it really means to believe that there is indeed one living God. Our Christian faith conviction of one God for all peoples in all places at all times is predicated by our response to the one living God of all creation. Paul's notion in Acts about God never being without witness (Acts 14:17) calls Asian Americans to view our own ethnicity with a prophetic eye. It calls us to recognize the signs of God's presence and activity in the whole of Asian American history, culture, and ethnicity, recognizing truth wherever we find it. "When our faith is expressed in familiar cultural modes which are well accepted by us, we speak of it as an *incarnation* of the faith," challenges Roy Sano, United Methodist Bishop of Southern California. He continues:

> [w]hen the cultural modes are unfamiliar, we are likely to speak of this embodiment of faith as syncretism. . . . I once asked myself: "How can I be Christian and yet Buddhist?" Through time, however, as I became aware of the extent to which Buddhism permeated my Japanese cultural heritage and recognized how impossible it was to eliminate everything from that heritage, my question changed. I now ask: "How can I be Christian without being Buddhist?" I do not mean this in the sense of formal membership in a religious body. I am speaking of a faithful articulation of the gospel through a cultural development in which the creative and providential, redeeming and hallowing care of God who is over all and in all has been at work.[47]

The issue here is a fundamental Christian belief in one God who made and who continues to make God-self known to humankind through Jesus Christ. This is to be recognized in every part of life for Asian Americans. We do not go on a large detour through European church history before we begin our own faith reflections. We need not go through all biblical and theological scholarship of the past, however much we might value it, in order to claim legitimacy for our own faith articulations. To be sure, the Bible still has a normative role. But it has a normative function precisely because what God did with the people of Israel, God's salvific activities, God continues to do with every people. The reason we would seek God in the Bible is in order to find God in our own lives. What is at stake for Asian Americans is not just a living and dynamic theology but a theology which is lived in community. The nature of Christian faith and theology must always be a response to the living God in the very concrete historical reality of our ethnicity embedded in our faith communities. Asian American churches' posture toward faith reflects this radically incarnational character of Christian faith.

Our culture evolves through the interaction of individual and collective memories with our daily experiences, forging new and distinct Asian American cultures. Born in the era of the Manifest Destiny, our churches have been subjected to the overwhelming forces of assimilation into the dominant culture of American society. And yet, paradoxically, we have remained for the most part "strangers and sojourners" in the household of God. Amidst the ambiguous dual role our churches have played for our people, our churches serve as an agent of emerging Asian American cultures incorporating elements of the collective memories and future visions of Asian Americans. Our churches are in this sense a primary setting for the emergence of new and distinct Asian American cultures, a place for us to meet the longing of our hearts and to forge a new sense of peoplehood. Christian faith takes on a crucial role in forming a community where we participate in common memory, community, and identity. There we find our place, our name, our story as Asian Americans.

Overcoming Invisibility: E Pluribus Unum Redefined

The emergence of new and distinct Asian American cultures amid our increasingly pluralistic society poses a new challenge to the definition of *e pluribus unum*. Ethnic pluralism as it developed in the United States in this century cannot plausibly be characterized as an antistate ideology or a reaction against the doctrine of sovereignty. Pluralism in our society does not challenge the authority of the federal government; it is not drawn to any of the forms of corporatism developed in Europe. It simply asserts that the coherence of society does not require cultural homogeneity, but rests on democratic citizenship. What had previously been understood as a temporary condition, the presence of diverse human groups in our society, is now demanding to be acknowledged as permanent. The United States is a society composed of many peoples. The very nature of this society, its new destiny, is to maintain diversity in a single coherence, without persecution or repression. Not only *from many, one*, but also *within one, many*.

Ethnic pluralism is one of the major challenges to the traditional argument for societal homogeneity. In a sense, ethnic self-assertion in the United States has been the functional equivalent of national liberation in other parts of the world. What are the actual functions that it serves? What does it mean to assert one's own ethnicity in a society whose very cohesiveness drives the assimilation and acculturization of diverse groups of people into an ideal shaped by a particular group of people, an ideal which prevails powerfully in today's society? These are also the questions Asian American churches are facing today as they strive to claim their visibility in society.

E pluribus unum—"from many, one"—became the visible slogan of our society in the 1840s and 1850s with the arrival of Irish immigrants who brought with them a vigorous and public Catholicism. At the same time came endless schisms and the birth of new religions—Unitarianism, Free Methodism, Mormonism. Protestant denominations divided North and South over the issues of the Civil War. Pluralism came to characterize the society and eventually falsified John Jay's account of its unity. The pluralism of our society is that of an immigrant society, which means that nationality and ethnicity never acquired a stable territorial base. Moreover, the minority groups were politically impotent and socially invisible during much of the time when American pluralism was taking shape—so the shape it has taken was not determined by their presence or by their repression.

What cohered the society was governmental, civic, and military in nature. Culturally, religiously, and for a time linguistically, they remained separate. "Churches, no longer made up of the whole community but only of the like-minded, became not so much pillars of public order as 'protected and withdrawn islands of piety,'" says Robert Bellah in his *Habits of the Heart*.[48] Religiously the society became diversified. Patriotism became the unifying force of society. "The voting booth is the temple of American institutions. No single tribe or family is chosen to watch the sacred fires burning on its altars . . . Each of us is a priest."[49] Patriotism served as an emotional and temporary unifying factor, a religion born of citizenship. But patriotism had an underlying assumption. Immigrants would one day constitute a single people united not only politically but also, in a deeper sense, by the ideal that has been in existence. This seems to be the meaning of *e pluribus unum* in the context of the emerging plurality in this society.

There are basically two ways to attain social coherence: gradual assimilation of racial/ethnic groups into the dominant culture, or the creation of an essentially new understanding of human relatedness, perhaps in the crucible of citizenship. The only alternatives, as the history of other nations has taught, are divisiveness, turmoil, and repression. Twentieth-century American history reveals that the fear of divisiveness, or simply of difference, periodically generated outbursts of anti-immigrant feeling among the European immigrants and their descendants. Limits on immigration, particularly against Asians, was one goal of these "nativist" campaigns. As early as 1882, the U.S. Congress passed the Chinese Exclusion Act, prohibiting further immigration of nearly all Chinese. In 1924 the federal government passed the Immigration Quota Act which, among other provisions, completely stopped all immigration from Japan. Asian immigrants were prohibited from owning land and real estate, were ineligible to apply for business licenses and citizenship, and forbidden to testify in court against European American persons. Another goal of the "nativist" campaign was the rapid Americanization of the "foreigners" and "strangers" already here. The cultural naturalization of Asians has proven to be difficult, however, for they are indeed "strangers from a foreign shore." They are perceived as aliens, unassimilable to American life, by agricultural and business interests, especially on the West Coast. Various legal and nonlegal means, such as humiliation, restrictions, and prohibitions, were used to keep Asian immigrants permanent aliens. The mass evacuation and internment of Japanese Americans was the most extreme case of such treatment.

In the face of the tide toward assimilation of racial/ethnic groups into the ideal of *e pluribus unum*, shaped and defined by the dominant European American culture, and the paradoxical exclusionist treatments against people of Asian descent, Asian Americans began gradually claiming visibility and demonstrating ethnic assertiveness. The challenge is redefining the basic underlying worldview of "from many, one." It is a movement to claim one's rightful place in the society of "within one, many."

> *We are here. We bring our memories and legacy. We bring our bamboo and rice. We bring our taro and palm. We bring our earth and ocean.*
>
> *We are here. We bring our struggles and hopes. We bring our shovels and picks to this land of opportunity. We bring our irons and ditches to this land of promise. We bring our broken hands and weeping hearts to this land of milk and honey.*
>
> *We are here. We bring our skills and our culture. We come to share and to care. We come to study and to teach. We have come to stay.*[50]

The first function of our ethnic assertiveness is the defense of our ethnicity against the pressures of cultural naturalization. Statistically, Asian Americans belong to the fastest-growing ethnic group in the United States. The Immigration Act of 1965 reopened the gates to Asian immigrants. In 1960, there were fewer than 900,000 people of Asian ancestry in the United States, representing a mere one-half of 1 percent of the country's population. In 1985, they numbered over five million, or 2.1 percent of the population. By the year 2000, Asian Americans are projected to make up 4 percent of the total U.S. population.

Furthermore, the pattern of Asian immigration has shifted. The new immigrants are basically two-generational groups, i.e., immigrant parents and their children. Sociologists Harry Kitano and Roger Daniels describe this new pattern, reflected in recent Korean immigrants: "[U]nlike the early Chinese, Japanese, and Filipinos, who came largely as individuals, Korean immigrants often arrived in family groups. . . . As a consequence, inter-generational differences in terms of acculturation, identity, language facility, and coming to grips with the dominant culture have an immediacy that was delayed for the older Asian groups."[51] For new Asian immigrants, generational terms often have not been useful to gauge the pattern of assimilation. The recent immigrants' ability to achieve a rapid acculturation to a new life in America does not necessarily repeat the same past pattern of melting into the dominant culture. At present, the bulk of young Koreans identify themselves as "one point fives," indicating that they were born in Korea but raised and educated in the United States. They tend to be bilingual and to embrace a much stronger Korean ethnic identity than their Japanese American counterparts. A new pattern of Korean American ethnicity is emerging.

Korean American churches serve as a vehicle toward the attainment of such ethnic visibility. They "score" more than perhaps any other Asian American church. They preach a stalwart Korean pride and a corporate Korean identity. Korean Americans' sense of identity is also closely linked to the Christian church. The Korean church also serves as a social and civic hub for their community. In stark contrast to the prevailing attitude in the Chinese and Japanese American communities, the Koreans view their pastors as people of high stature and prominence. "If you want to make me proud of you, become either a doctor, a lawyer, or a pastor," encourages a non-Christian father to his son. Ethnic coherence runs high in the new wave of Korean Americans in their churches.

A notable sign of this newly emerging ethnic visibility and assertiveness among Korean and other Asian American Christians is that of collective identity in place of individual selfhood. Most often, when individual Asian Americans insist on "being ourselves," we are in fact defending a self we share with others. Sometimes we succumb and learn to conform to standardized versions of New World behavior. Or we wait, frightened and passive, for organizational support from groups such as the Asian American Caucus of the United Methodist Church or the Pacific and Asian American Ministries of the United Church of Christ. When such organizations go to work, our form of the struggle for visibility is plain to see, even if arguments continue to focus on individual rights. "The caucus movement is primarily to affirm the identity of a people. . . . [T]hrough the movement we can celebrate the richness and joy of yellow and brown Christian faith," says Jonah Chang, speaking about the history of the National Federation of Asian American United Methodists.[52] The resolution passed by the Asian American Caucus of the United Methodist Church in 1971 speaks of its objectives:

1. Self-determination to develop relevant Christian mission strategies on the local, annual conference, and national levels.
2. Openness to explore and to appreciate the values of our ethnic, cultural, and religious heritages that make the gospel relevant and meaningful to Asian Americans.
3. Liberation from the elements of racism within the United Methodist Church and society.

While the language reflects the activist sentiments of the era, the resolution nevertheless expresses the caucus's concerns with their collective identity. "Although unable to fill all the needs of Asian American United Methodists, the caucus has been an effective alternative by which persons could participate in the United Methodist Church," says Jonah Chang.[53]

Another example of the Asian American collective ethnic

assertion began in a small United Methodist Church on Chicago's north side, Parish of the Holy Covenant. The Parish has an illustrious history of involvement in the movements for civil rights, peace, and women's rights. In January 1979, the congregation, with only five Japanese Americans among its members, decided to support the redress initiative taken by the Japanese American Citizens League (JACL) against the injustice of the internment of Japanese Americans during World War II. The Parish's strategy was to work through the Northern Illinois Annual Conference of the United Methodist Church and to do grassroots lobbying for whatever redress legislation the JACL might propose.

In March 1979 the JACL altered its course and moved to initiate a study. The congregation felt uneasy because it sensed that enough study had been done. It decided to embark upon its own, more direct course of action. The decision resulted in launching a national movement, the National Council for Japanese American Redress (NCJAR). Along with a coalition in Seattle known as the Seattle Redress Committee, NCJAR assisted Rep. Mike Lowry of the State of Washington in introducing a redress bill in November 1979. In the meantime, strongly worded resolutions on redress had been passed in three annual conferences of the United Methodist Church—Northern Illinois, Pacific Northwest, and Oregon-Idaho. The Northern Illinois resolution was also submitted as a petition to the 1980 General Conference of the United Methodist Church.

Even though the redress bill was eventually substituted by the establishment of a study commission, it paved the way toward the ultimate passage of the Redress Bill in the Congress in 1988. Finally, the victims of what Congressman Robert Matsui terms "a collective rape" spoke out at the hearings. "The former internees finally had spoken, and their voices compelled the nation to redress the injustice of internment," says Ronald Takaki.[54]

If the first function of Asian American ethnic assertiveness is the defense of ethnicity against cultural naturalization, the second function is the celebration of our collective identity. Celebration is critical to our claim for visibility because the pressures for assimilation work to undermine communal confidence. Asian Americans find it necessary to group together for mutual support and acceptance when denied access to mainstream America. Bazaars, ethnic festivals, and the like are ways of coping with the sense of isolation and marginalization associated with immigration into U.S. society. "Whether by choice or by force, once drawn together, Asians developed communities which mirrored in miniature the life they knew in Asia. Asian social structures, organizations, and modes of interaction were re-created and traditional customs were sustained, although much was modified in adaptation to the new land."[55] To survive, we have drawn on our memories of cultural values to create new social structures which in turn, have become expressions of Asian American culture. In the same way, we have also created a variety of celebrative events to respond to needs unmet by the wider American society.

> We organized the group called Daughters of the Philippines with about 25 or 30 of us girls who took an active part in the Filipino Community. We did all kinds of things like put on celebrations. . . . These social events were important to the Filipino Community, a necessity. Imagine a life where you are more or less kept to yourselves. We weren't welcome in many public places. So all the social affairs that you could go to were those that you'd have to plan yourselves. These were even more important for all these single men who were alone because there were hardly any women that came with them from the Philippines.[56]

In these early expressions of Asian American culture, today's cultural festivals, community events, and various ethnic organizations have their roots. With each successive generation, the needs and memories of a people change, and new expressions of culture evolve.

Bazaars are particularly noteworthy for the celebration of the history and culture of Japanese American Christians.

> On the day before the Bazaar, men and women customarily come together and prepare the chickens. Waking before dawn, on the morning of the Bazaar, men gather to prepare the bar-

becue pits, and then go through their annual ritual of cooking the chickens to be served later that day. The aroma of "chicken teriyaki" fills the air, and time for the celebration soon begins. The sacrifice of the chickens, the ritual cooking is complete, and the feasting will soon begin. People will gather in reaffirmation of who they are at a place, the church, which serves to not only preserve their story, but transforms their very being.[57]

Ethnic celebration is the celebration of diversity itself, the celebration of the history and culture of a particular group. The former would be meaningless without the latter, for otherwise the celebration of diversity would remain abstract, without the vitality of concrete embodiment. Diversity in itself has no powers of survival. It depends upon energy, enthusiasm, and commitment within the component groups and cannot outlast the particularity of cultures and ethnicities. We celebrate our ethnic particularities not only because they are distinct and exciting; our celebration is that our ethnicities provide the framework and perspective to enable us to see the reality of life clearly and to motivate us to engage in the civic life in the society. The celebration of ethnicity creates a doorway into the world rather than an escape out of the world.

The third function of ethnic assertiveness is to build and sustain the reborn community—to create institutions, gain control of resources, and provide educational and welfare services. This is hard work, and there is a difficulty peculiar to ethnic groups in an increasingly pluralist society; such groups do not have coercive authority over their members—they have no guaranteed population. Though they are historical communities, they must function as if they were voluntary associations. They must make ethnicity a conscious goal. They need to persuade people to "ethnicize" rather than Americanize themselves. Any group that hopes to survive must commit itself to the same pattern of activity—winning support, fund-raising, forming community activities, and caring for the elderly. Religion is a powerful cohering force for this purpose and churches are particularly suited for this expression of ethnic assertiveness.

The Chinese Methodist Center Corporation (CMCC) is an outreach ministry of New York City's Chinese United Methodist Church, located in the heart of Chinatown. CMCC is a bustling center of church community activity. It is a place that "never sleeps . . . something is always going on in this place," observes a board member. CMCC serves some five hundred to six hundred children, youth, and adults in the Chinatown community each week in a variety of programs, including a five-day after-school program, youth action group, and immigrant counseling.

Strengthening the family by improving communications is one of the goals of CMCC. The Mei Wah School, one of the CMCC programs, has become a key force seeking to close this communication gap. "We are trying to help the generations build a bridge towards each other," Jackson T. W. Lee, principal of the school, explains. Most parents have limited facility with the English language, while their children speak little or no Chinese. Language is not the only barrier dividing families. Many parents work extremely long hours and young people are left with lots of time on their hands. Through a comprehensive program of education and recreation for youth, CMCC tries to teach young people to assume responsibility and make good use of their time.

The Youth Action Group, the primary vehicle for leadership training, organizes community service projects and sponsors recreational activities for young people in the community. Group and individual counseling is available for youth to discuss personal, college, and career issues. Youth director Mary Hsu explains that the workshop on mental health was particularly important because of the stigma attached to any type of mental illness in the Chinese community. Although the Chinese have the highest suicide rate in New York City, families try to hide it when suicide directly affects them.

When we asked the question that Jesus asked, "Who is my neighbor?" Ming Guy Quock, president of the board, responds, "The answer was clear: Our neighbors were youngsters, who needed to know the rich heritage and language of their ancestors; they were working parents, who were desperate for a place to send their preschool children; they were new immigrants, young and old, whose inability to speak English was holding them back from achieving their dreams in a new land; and they were teen-agers, who had no place to go and nothing to do and who yearned for a way to channel their creative energies. . . . Our vision was to provide a community center . . . where people of all ages could find help for some of these pressing needs."

Building and sustaining one's community is the practice of empowerment. Since the 1960s, Asian American churches have been experiencing an empowered position, rather than mere visi-bility, within the social structures. Political awareness gradually began to emerge in the process of Asian American ethnic asser-tiveness. This is particularly true in Asian American Christians' claim for their place within Protestant denominational struc-tures. But here, too, the enormity of the power of assimilation is revealed. Asian American intellectuals, including church leaders, have found themselves in tension between their desire to move into the dominant social, political, and economic struc-tures of society and their need for an ethnic power base that would serve as an anchoring point within the society (but which was not readily available to them). In the United Methodist denomination, Taro Goto in 1948 became the first district super-intendent of Japanese ancestry and remained the only superin-tendent of the Japanese Provisional Annual Conference for a long time.

The reasons for this bind for Asian American Christians lie in several areas. First, the church leaders serve a core of active participants within the community, but there also exists a much larger periphery of people who are little more than occasional recipients of services generated by their leaders. This periphery group, furthermore, dilutes the denominational boundaries. The crossover of Asian American Christians among denominations is quite extensive. There is really no way for the various groups to prevent or regulate individual crossings. Thus the leaders are generally distanced from the very group of people they are sup-posed to represent.

Second, this distance is reinforced by attempts on the part of denominational bodies to include ethnic representation in their leadership. In order to guarantee such representation, it is not necessary for the ethnic churches to organize and choose their own spokespersons. Educational training, social visibility, and other personal factors often play a more significant role in ethnic leadership in denominational and ecumenical circles than status within respective ethnic groups. Leaders from ethnic groups tend to stand in no political relationship to their groups. They are not responsible agents, nor are they bound to speak for the interests of their ethnic or religious groups. In this way, even affirmative action provides opportunities to individuals without granting a voice to groups. It serves to enhance the visibility and status of individuals, not necessarily the resources of the ethnic community.

In one form or another, Asian American church leadership is in a tenuous state: Though it would be necessary for individuals to identify themselves (or to be identified) as group members in order to make fair representation of Asian American Christian communities, this identification does not necessarily point to the representation of the communities themselves. While this situation is changing with the gradual increase in the appointments of such representative figures as Bishop Wilbur Choy and Roy Sano of the United Methodist Church, Mineo Katagiri, Teruo Kawata, and David Hirano as Conference Ministers of the United Methodist Church (Dr. Hirano now heads the Board for World Ministries of the United Church of Christ), the impact of Asian American leadership is still limited. Ethnic empowerment within a larger group, reflected in the ecclesial structure of Protestant denominations, often mitigates ethnic representation and once again opens the co-opting of Asian American leaders into the prevailing or evolving culture of the larger society. Once again, this points to the fundamental dilemma of empowerment reflected in the current state of Asian American church leadership. The assertiveness of our ethnicities remains a difficult challenge.

The early history of Asian American churches is characterized by their attempt to claim their own place in a society that thought cohesiveness depended upon an assimilation and homogeneity, a worldview developed by a particular group of people who occupied the dominant role in society. However, the eventual shift in the ethnic makeup of society due to increased immigration, particularly from Asia, challenged the underlying assumption of the cultural homogeneity of *e pluribus unum*. The gradual rise in the ethnic assertion of various groups of color also made this worldview difficult to sustain. Ethnic pluralism challenges U.S. society to move beyond "from many, one" to the vision of "within one, many." Maxine Hong Kingston talks about what it means to "claim America":

> Does "claiming America" mean assimilation of American values? No. I mean it as a response to the legislation and racism that says we of Chinese origin do not belong here in America. It's a response to the assumption that I come from Vietnam or another Asian country. When I say that I am a native American with all the rights of an American, I am saying, "No, we're not outsiders; we Chinese belong here. This is our country, this is our history, we are a part of America. If it weren't for us, America would be a different place." [58]

Is the vision of "within one, many," a sustainable vision in this society that is experiencing the brutalization of various ethnic communities, as painfully illustrated in the Los Angeles riots of 1992? Will the heightened ethnic assertiveness on the part of Asian Americans contribute to the fragmentation and Balkanization of different human groups in society? Or will it participate in creating a new way of relating one with another? Asian American churches exist amid such difficult questions facing all the people of this nation.

The Quest for a Different Way of Human Relatedness

People look to some form of community for support, comfort, and a sense of belonging, while for freedom, fairness, and justice they look to the society at large. This is no less true with Asian Americans: we are communal in our personal affairs and collaborative in our politics. While our ethnic communities, including churches, nurture our sense of identity and provide us with a framework of meaning, political realities force us into alliances with other groups to ensure fair and just representation in society. The democratic process recognizes each person as the equal of every other, without regard to ethnicity, and fosters a solidarity of individuals alongside the diversity of groups. Increasingly, Asian Americans are becoming conscious of the importance of such alliances and coalitions in order to claim our own place in society. Our churches are no exception to this trend. Some Asian American Christians seek in denominations and the wider churches a new sense of Asian American collective identity, beyond ancestral and historical boundaries. Others resort to a clearly drawn sense of individual ethnicity for such identity. "History has proven that at a most crucial point, the United Methodist church did not respond to its missional tasks," says Jonah Chang, a former United Methodist superintendent, commenting on that denomination's policy of integration that resulted in the mergers of provisional conferences with regular conferences in late 1950s and middle 1960s.[59] In response to the denomination's failure to honor the representation of Asian American groups, the National Federation of Asian American United Methodists was eventually formed in 1975. A new sense of Asian American collective ethnicity was born within the United Methodist church.

Similar movements are also taking place elsewhere. "I consider myself neither Korean or any other Asian. I am a Hawaiian," says Colleen Chun, a third-generation Korean American United Methodist pastor in Honolulu. She is one of the last in her generation to be born between two Korean parents. "After second generation, a total diffusion took place." This is a representative response heard among people of Asian ancestry in Hawaii. There is a strong sense of "Hawaiian" identity among Christians in Hawaii. Community Church of Honolulu, which began as a Chinese American congregation in 1906, now prides itself as a community church that is "supra-racial and supra-national, open to all, regardless of race, class, or caste, and seeks to render a real service to the community in the light of its needs."[60] Even though the ethnic makeup of the congregation is still predominantly Chinese American (approximately 75 percent), people of Japanese, Korean, and European American ancestries are also among its members. Early in its history the church decided not to use the Chinese language in its worship services, but the Hawaiian language was incorporated into English, which serves as the primary language of communication. "Give everybody the freedom to express themselves, and the freedom to listen to a new interpretation. But everybody's got to respect each other and be more broad-minded. And see if we can work together," says founding leader Hung Wai Ching.[61] The earlier attempt to move away from the Chinese American ethnic identity to a more inclusive identity was likely due to the church's desire to become more assimilated into the "American" culture. It is reflected in their choice of the name "Community Church of Honolulu." As the younger generation of Chinese Americans began to fill the pews, however, the need for assimilation was no longer a primary concern for the church. What holds the church together is now shifted to certain values that its people cherish together, such as family relationships and respect for one another. Can these and other cherished values sustain the church for the future in a society that is more ethnically diverse than many other parts of the United States? How is the changing scene of peoplehood in the Community Church of Honolulu lived out as their experience of Christian faith? These are the challenges facing this particular faith community.

The current discussion on Hawaiian sovereignty among churches in Hawaii reflects this "supra-ethnic" or "pan-ethnic" identity of people of Asian descent in Hawaii. The resolution titled "Recognizing the Right to Self Governance of Native Hawaiians," submitted by Tuck Wah Lee and Kaelo Patterson of the United Church of Christ in 1990 and supported by the State Council of Hawaiian Churches, represents a milestone. But the picture is still unclear. It appears that ethnic churches continue to flourish side by side in Hawaii with those moving toward a more ethnically inclusive pattern of community life.

On the ecumenical scene, Asian Americans are also beginning to express themselves cooperatively. Since the 1970s a number of Asian American ministers have been involved in national agencies that explore and develop strategies for the field of Asian and Pacific American theology. These agencies include the Episcopal Church's Asiamerica Ministry, the Pacific and Asian American Ministry of the United Church of Christ, the Asian Mission Development Office of the Presbyterian Church U.S.A., the Pacific and Asian American Center for Theology and Strategies (PACTS), and numerous others. An emerging collective Asian American Christian identity is reflected in these endeavors: "[T]here is a growing sense that there is something Asian-American about the experience which we have shared in the United States. We certainly don't yet know about each other's particular experiences but there is growing willingness to understand what other Asian-Americans have experienced and to discover together what it is that has given shape to our common experience as Asian-American."[62]

Another expression of evolving ethnic consciousness comes from the statistical evidence of cross-ethnic "out-marriages" among Asian Americans, resulting in a further merging or melting into the dominant group. In Los Angeles County, in 1977, the records indicate 60 percent of Japanese, 49.7 percent of Chinese, and 34.1 percent of Koreans marrying outside their ethnic groups. Though the percentage has dropped slightly since 1977, perhaps due to the growing incidence of new immigrants in the Asian American population, the actual number of out-marriages has been increasing since then.[63] The trend toward marrying outside one's racial and ethnic group is a strong indicator of the degree to which that ethnic group is assimilating into the dominant cultural group in society. "When you can accept intermarriage, when a group freely intermarries with the dominant group, that group can be said to be assimilated," says Edgar Epps, a race relations authority and professor of urban education at the University of Chicago. Sansei Japanese American poet Ron Tanaka asserts that the sansei are fast losing their identity as Japanese Americans, becoming instead simply "non-Anglo": "We are, for the most part, no longer a community in the sense of a group of people who live, work, and play together. We have our communities to join the mainstream. . . . we have 'out-whited' the whites and hence ceased to be what we are."[64] While this dismal picture may not be representative of the Japanese American population as a whole, it does speak of a trend that can no longer be ignored.

Individual freedom and mobility are special values but also the characteristic weakness of American pluralism. They generate a world without boundaries. In that world, the vitality of a given ethnic group is tested by its ability to hold onto people in various dimensions of life and to shape their self-images and their convictions. Kitano and Daniels observe that "[t]he assimilation variable . . . includes integration into the schools, the work place, the social groupings, as well as identification with the majority and marital assimilation. The ethnic identity dimension is essentially a pluralistic adaptation, focusing on the retention of ethnic ways," in each of these dimensions of life.[65] The high rate of out-marriage among Asian Americans rapidly facilitates our assimilation into the cultural mainstream. Churches are not immune to this trend. "Japanese American pastors are an endangered species," says Masaru Nambu, pastor of a Japanese American Baptist congregation in Chicago. Such a comment reflects the diminishing sizes of most of Japanese American mainline Protestant congregations. While the picture is not as discouraging for the other three ancestral groups (Chinese, Filipino, and Korean), the gradual waning of Japanese American congregations does not present a hopeful sign for the overall Asian American church scene.

Ethnic boundaries are difficult to draw. There is no way for the various groups to prevent or regulate individual crossings. Ethnicity is always fluid, dynamic, and evolving. Racial and ethnic identities derive their meanings from social and historical circumstances and they can vary over time. Wesley Woo of Presbyterian Church, U.S.A., observes: "In the late '60s we were fairly definite about this [Asian American] identity—particularly as a political statement. It is now becoming a cultural statement as well. But, at the same time, an authentic Asian- or Pacific-Asian American collective identity is more fragile today."[66] This survey of Asian American Protestant churches confirms a multifaceted picture of Asian American ethnicity. There are both the rise of collective identity and the continuing assertion of individual ethnicity among various groups. These are happening simultaneously in the face of increasing cross-ethnic marriages among Asian Americans.

In the fluid Asian American ethnic scene, what is at stake is the availability of opportunities for fair and just group representation without any requirement of ethnic boundary and organization. What is needed is for all people, without reference to their groups, to share more or less equally in the resources of American life. Beyond that, distributive justice among groups is bound to be relative to the vitality of their centers and committed members. Ultimately each group determines its own coherence and life.

While the matter of ethnicity is multifaceted, a common thread runs through the history and development of Asian American churches. We find ourselves in an untenable position between the ever-present reminder of our "racial uniform," which isolates us from full participation in society, and equally powerful forces toward acculturation into the dominant European American culture. Both the heightened sense of ethnic awareness among Asian American churches and the emerging collective identity among Asian American church leaders is fueled internally by the widespread loss of confidence in American society and externally by the changed cultural relationships of Asian American groups. "Unfortunately, many non-Asians have difficulty understanding or accepting this 'Asian American' identity. Many . . . think that Asians can only be one of two kinds—they are either 'Asians' (i.e., immigrant) through and through or they are essentially 'American' (i.e., totally assimilated and acculturated)."[67] This is a typical experience of Asian Americans. We have become ethnically self-conscious enough to call into question the viability of traditional American society and its ability to understand our ethnicity. This is in part because the broadly Protestant hegemony of European American culture is experienced as alien and oppressive. But what holds the whole society together in its stead? Alasdair MacIntyre argues that "those of us in America who come together do so from a variety of pasts and variety of stories to tell. If we do not recover and identify with the particularities of our own community, then we shall lose what it is that we have to contribute to the common culture. We shall have nothing to bring, nothing to give. But if each of us dwells too much, or even exclusively, upon his or her own ethnic particularity, then we are in danger of fragmenting and even destroying the common life." And yet, for those who have been confined in what Ron Takaki terms "iron cages," the term coined by Max Weber, where one's emotions are controlled and one's spirit subdued, the term "common life" is an alien concept.

The real issue for Asian Americans has less to do with the "common life" for people of this society and more to do with the common and "shared sense of pathos and tragedy" among us.[68] "Pacific and Asian-Americans are . . . a people with 'pathos'— with stories of deep pain and suffering. A primary source of this pathos is to be found in the racism encountered in America," says Wesley Woo.[69] This is particularly pronounced in the experiences of Asian immigrant women. In the late 1800s and early 1900s, many of the Chinese and Japanese women in this country were prostitutes, brought into this country through the luring, kidnapping, and trading activities of Asian importers and brothel owners. The average Chinese prostitute was indentured for four to five years without wages. While this practice no longer occurs, the plight of Asian immigrant women continues. Because of the discrimination experienced by Asian American men and the resulting low wages and frequent changes in employment, the percentage of Asian American women who work is much higher than that of European American women, and they receive lower pay. As a result of sexual, economic, and racial discrimination, they are some of the most overqualified, underskilled workers. As garment and jewelry factory employees, hotel maids, nurses' aides, and clerks, their incomes are scarcely enough to cover individual and family necessities.

This shared sense of pathos and tragedy serves as the basic framework for Asian American ethnicity, both in its national ancestry forms and in a more inclusive collective expression. Ethnicity, in other words, is much more than a set of cultural traits of a given group. It is more accurately understood as a symbol of group identity and history, and as the seed for the creation of community.

This shared experience of pain and suffering may indeed hold the key to the basic relatedness of all people. Seen from the perspective of Asian Americans, what holds American society together has little to do with the idea of unity often defined philosophically in Western culture as *e pluribus unum*. Rather, it has to do with painful experiences of alienation and estrangement among human beings individually and collectively. The pain and suffering of alienation do not necessarily produce a sense of community. Rather, such experiences can create a setting in which alternative ways of relating with others become possible, ways centered in reconciliation rather than estrangement. Since the early part of this century, rising consumerism, suburbanization, out-marriage, and a host of other social and cultural factors have helped create a profound homogeneity among Asian Americans. Yet a sense of ethnic awareness continues to exist among us primarily because of our undeniable experiences of pain and suffering. Our responses, often nonviolent, to this pain and tragedy are the creation of the beloved community. This community distinguishes us not only from other ethnic groups but, more important, from the monolithic, cross-ethnic, middle-class culture that has imposed the suffering upon Asian Americans and others. Given this shared experience of pain and suffering, ethnic identity for Asian Americans expresses our own history, social structure, and emotional relations. This identity becomes a vehicle by which traditions are passed from one generation to another, contributing to the emergence of a yet new and distinct culture. Churches are the primary locus for this to take place. Will this new cultural coherence among Asian American Christians perpetuate the existing pattern of domination and subordination among various ethnic and cultural groups in our society? Or will it participate in forging a new pattern of human relatedness that respects the dignity and worth of every ethnic group? The future of Asian American churches rests in part on this challenge.

The gift of the gospel is a gift of courage to see the world for what it is. Churches have served as an important arena for Asian Americans to find our own places in a world that often threatens to deny our own identity. The church is a community where we have freedom to quest for the longing of our heart. It is the place where we have the freedom to refuse to behave according to the rules set by another cultural group. Church is the place where we take an active role in determining our own ways of relating to the rest of society and particularly to those who control the agenda of society. Membership in the churches has given us a vision of a reality that transcends the limits imposed by the society, a vision that enables us to be honest about ourselves, about our fears and hopes. Such a vision is that of reconciled humanity. To be sure, the simple proclamation of the gospel of reconciliation is not enough to effect the needed liberation from the power of domination of one group over others. What is at stake is "the basic form of humanity," as Karl Barth calls it, or humanity in encounter. Being in encounter can never happen authentically when oppression and domination block the fulfillment of human relatedness. The choice between the distortion and ruin or the awakening and fulfillment of a multiethnic society turns on this fact. The failure of a multiethnic society can easily result in violent co-annihilation, as was suggested by the Los Angeles riots. The awakening and fulfillment of multiethnic humanity correlates with this. However it is construed, whether by the gospel of Jesus Christ or by any other attempt to realize ultimate human worth and dignity, this fulfillment must either await or accompany the removal of domination and oppression. For Asian American Christians, the solidarity of people within the community of faith provides a viable means of challenging oppression. In the context of the church and its struggle to claim its own place in society is the gospel heard as the gospel for all.

The churches have given us courage to confront the world on our own terms, in other words. By its very existence, the church provides us with an imaginative alternative for society and the freedom to forge our own identity. The chief political task of the Asian American church is not to provide suggestions for social policy but to be in our very existence a social policy. The church is struggling to create those structures that this society has not been able to achieve. American society as it stands cannot achieve justice, freedom, and community. The real validation of the Jesus story is when the world looks at us and says, as it said of our forebears in the faith, "See how they love one another."

Churches for us are indeed *ecclesia semper reformanda*, a community forming and reforming. We are always en route, our eyes always looking for that new city that God is building among us (Heb. 11). The relationship between ethnicity and faith rests in the nature of the church as lived out within Asian American Christian communities. Ecclesia functions to reform and transform the community, giving us a new level of awareness of who we are and where we are in this society, ultimately redefining the notion of *e pluribus unum*, "from many, one," to "within one, many." The heart of the issue here is the nature of community. Faith community is for Asian American Christians the center of our existence in this society. It is a primary setting in which our relationships with other ethnic and cultural groups are experienced and understood. Furthermore, the vitality of our faith communities is to be tested by its ability to hold onto those who are not directly related to the faith community, and to help shape their self-images and their convictions. The lives of the people on the periphery of the church are enhanced by this community which they do not actively support and by an identity they need not themselves cultivate. There is no way to charge them for what they receive from the church. But their most important gain may be nothing more than a certain sense of pride, an aura of ethnicity, otherwise unavailable. The church's very existence depends on those who benefit from our struggles and accomplishments. This is the very nature of Christian community, and it is incarnated in Asian American churches.

≋ 2

Holy Insecurity
Asian American Faith Quest for Identity

[A]s Asian American Christians we stand on the various boundaries which are our lot: between Asia and America; rural and
urban; intuitive thought and rational logic; . . . minority and
majority; non-white and white . . . It is the audacity of the
Asian American Christian, and those others in the Christian
community who would join us, to affirm that the happening at
the margin and the boundary are truly the center and the opening
into the future of a life affirming humanity." [1]

Asian Americans are caught in a web of assimilation that will
not easily let us go. Like all immigrants and refugees before us, we
inexorably find ourselves on a common road to assimilation. Our
claim for Asian American cultural or ethnic distinctness is often
incompatible with the powerful thrust toward homogeneity
which prevails powerfully within U.S. society. There is also a
troubling sense among Asian Americans that we will remain a
"minor key," irrelevant, or worse, an obstruction, to the society
even if we go along with the prevailing tide. We live in what
Harvard sociologist William Greenbaum terms "the North
American contradiction," a universalism made up of ethnic, cul-

tural, religious, and sexual exclusions of those who do not fit into the dominant norm of the society.[2] This awareness is exacerbated by the fact that a greater American collective identity is yet to emerge in this increasingly pluralistic society. This is due largely to the fact that there is no shared history or religion that joins people together, save perhaps the voting booth ("the temple of American institutions," as Supreme Court Justice David Brewer wrote in 1900). Even the door of this temple was not open to Asian Americans until recently. Here lies the deepest spiritual pain of pluralism in America, an absence of the glue that holds all people together.

To compound the problem, we Asian Americans find ourselves in a liminal world that is cultural and linguistic, as well as cross-generational, in character. A liminal world is the "place of in-betweenness." It is at once the world of isolation and intimacy, desolation and creativity. A person in a liminal world is poised in uncertainty and ambiguity between two or more social constructs, reflecting in the soul the discords and harmonies, repulsions and attractions. One of the constructs is likely to be dominant, whether cultural or linguistic. Within such a dominant construct one strives to belong and yet finds oneself to be a peripheral member, forced to remain in the world of in-betweenness.

The shifting gender roles and relationships between Asian American women and men are also increasingly becoming a significant factor contributing to this liminality, because of the rise in gender awareness and assertiveness by women in general. "Our conversations are constantly in danger of getting polarized in terms of who is right and who is wrong, what each is due, and who is innocent. These conflicts must help us think in more complex and wise ways about how bodies and experiences create different kinds of gender, so that we see the limits to 'woman,' as white feminists have defined that term, just as they claim that there are limits to 'human,' as white men have defined that reality," says theologian Rita Nakashima Brock.[3] These and other liminal factors that Asian Americans experience make the definition of our identities increasingly difficult. We find ourselves within a new, dynamic, and ambiguous situation, betwixt and between all fixed points of classification. We have reached a kind of geographical, cultural, and political margin where old norms have become detached, and we find ourselves groping for new associations and new enterprises. How do Christian faith experiences in our communities of faith respond to the identity concerns of Asian Americans? In this chapter the subject of both personal and collective Asian American identity is treated in light of our experience of liminality and the heritage of Christian faith.

Asian Americans' ethnically and culturally liminal states are often voiced as significant factors affecting our identities. "I'm afraid I'm losing my Korean-American culture. I have an almost dual identity as a Korean Presbyterian, and at Northwestern, there is not a large Korean community that can relate to this," a Korean student, Arnold Park says. "We've been inundated by our parents all our lives: Keep your history, keep your language, keep your culture."[4] Park finds such a monocultural identity impossible to retain. Sam Hayakawa, no favorite authority figure of many Asian Americans, nonetheless accurately noted: "The more they [the sansei] rejected quietness, conformity, discipline, and the stereotype of the well-behaved Japanese . . . the farther they got from their cultural roots." This sober realization is reflected in various areas of Asian American activities, particularly in the contemporary literary and film arts fields, whose tenor is one of introspection and profound angst over identities. The plot of *Living on Tokyo Time*, a film directed and cowritten by Steven Okazaki, mirrors this concern. Ken, a sansei, does not have much in common with his parents, but he has even less in common with his live-in woman friend Kyoko, who has recently arrived from Japan. A definitive anti-Yuppie, he doesn't even like Japanese food. He is forced to go his own way and learn who he is without bogus cultural props. He's an American with a Japanese face, a broken heart, a guitar, and a life to live. Eventually, after a painful soul search he comes to the realization that life means accepting all of those contradictions, and not running from the Japanese face.

multiple
identity

Questions arise out of the profound anxiety of Asian Americans over our identities. Should ethnicity be a primary factor for our identities in this society? Do we look to another source in order to claim our identities? If it is not possible to ignore our ethnicities, what provides us with our primary anchoring points? Can we rely on our ancestral cultural heritages for our identity? What is the relationship between the particularity of being, for instance, Chinese American, and the commonality of being Asian American, or being a member of this society as a whole? What should one do in the situation in which a person says, "I'm American," while the rest of the society is saying, "You are Asian"? How should we reconcile individual rights to identify ourselves with a sense of a collective peoplehood? What is the glue that holds us together? These are the questions confronted by Asian Americans.

The Pain and Promise of Pluralism

This society stands at the meeting point of a number of different histories, each of them the bearer of a highly particular tradition, each of those traditions to a large degree mutilated, fragmented, and transmutated by its encounter with others. The North American "common life" is really a life of encounter for rival and often incompatible values and perspectives. Arthur Schlesinger warns of the rise of the "cult of ethnicity," which threatens to tear apart the very fabric of American society: "Instead of a nation composed of individuals making their own free choices, America increasingly sees itself as composed of groups more or less indelible in their ethnic character. The national ideal had once been *e pluribus unum*. Are we now to belittle *unum* and glorify *pluribus*? Will the center hold? Or will the melting pot yield to the Tower of Babel?"[5]

While Schlesinger's observation may reflect the concern and fear of the norm-setting dominant group, American society has not readily recognized the implications of the deep differences among various groups, ethnic or otherwise, nor has it examined the distortions that result from misnaming them and their effects on human behavior and expectation. What are the underlying assumptions behind the "*unum*"? Who defines it? Historically when a dominant group has wished to subjugate a certain group of people in this society in the name of unity, it has first made them subhuman. In 1850, Louis Agassiz, professor of natural history at Harvard, characterized African Americans and Native Americans respectively as "the submissive, obsequious negro" and the "indomitable, courageous, proud Indian," who, he claimed, were obviously no match culturally for European Americans, who are the "learned classifier."[6] As for Asian Americans, Filipinos were viewed by the newspaper media in the late nineteenth and early twentieth centuries as "scarcely more than savages" and Chinese "nagurs."[7] Here is assembled a great, troubling disturbance about a "high" culture that has itself come to be seen as a source of alienation and estrangement by various groups precisely in its claim to its own superiority. When a differentiation is perceived in terms of the domination and subjugation of others, the search for a commonality is likely to become self-protective and competitive rather than communally based and collectively shared. In such a societal setting, the "unity" means the protection of the dominant group and its culture rather than a representational and mutual sharing of "life-together."

In a society with the presence of a powerful group dominating others, the issue of identity for Asian Americans has little to do with the Cartesian notion of "clear and distinct ideas" about our individual personality traits or ethnic and cultural distinctness. Rather it is influenced by our ways of coping with the societal perception of our "deviant" status on the part of the dominant cultural group, as Audrey Lorde states in *Sister Outsider*.[8] "Too often, we pour the energy needed for recognizing and exploring difference into pretending those differences are insurmountable barriers, or that they do not exist at all. This results in a voluntary isolation, or false and treacherous connections. Either way, we do not develop tools for using human difference as a springboard for creative change within our lives. We speak not of human difference, but of human deviance," Lorde argues.[9]

Certainly there are very real differences among various groups. But it is not those differences that are the source of our identity concerns. It is rather a claim for the inherent superiority of the dominant cultural and ethnic group over all others that creates the setting in which Asian Americans, along with other people of color, are forced to grapple with our existence in this society. Our very beings, ethnically and culturally, are perceived as deviating from the norm set by the dominant cultural and ethnic group.

The alienating posture of the dominant cultural group toward Asian Americans and other racial/ethnic groups results primarily from its refusal both to recognize the damaging effect of such a claim of superiority and to examine the distortions which result from the claim. As long as the perceived deviance of Asian Americans and other racial and ethnic groups exists, our quest for identity is affected by our painful experience of estrangement from the mainstream society.

Survival and dignity for Asian Americans, both individuals and groups, are thus at stake. "You are a homeless dog without your identity. Though we are U.S. citizens, we are Japanese. The color of our faces and so on. . . . Losing identity is the same as losing money; you lose your way of life," laments a first-generation Japanese immigrant.[10] Asian Americans are inevitably conditioned by the self-accrediting act of rational consciousness shaped within Western Enlightenment modernity. However, the matter of Asian American self-identity is more accurately understood through our ability to cope with an often inhospitable society and to locate our own sense of dignity and worth within it. Such strife inevitably leads us toward a quest for a fair and just order in society where each group of people, whether it is an ethnic, cultural, gender, religious, or lifestyle group, will have fair and equal representation and treatment. The quest of Asian Americans for identity, particularly as seen from our Christian faith perspective, is no less than our affirmation of the justice and peace and integrity of the whole created order.

Moreover, our search for identity is likely to be expressed not so much in individualistic fashion as in a communally shared expression of peoplehood among Asian Americans. Though raised within the highly individualistic, male-dominated North American environment, Asian Americans are nevertheless unwilling to draw strict boundaries between the self and others, boundaries likely to promote a sense of isolation among our people. This is particularly true for first-generation immigrants. We can find in our history examples of how the notion of self as personal power in relationship to others is avoided.

Take, for example, the history of Chinese Americans. Racist legislation limited immigration, creating communities with bachelor populations. Elaine Kim of the University of California at Berkeley describes how the absence of women and traditional family life led to the development of an organizational network which became a substitute for family life and the establishment of a collective Chinese American identity: "Bound together by their social status as a despised minority, tied by tradition and common beliefs and interests, the Chinese immigrants constructed a world based on social solidarity between families and clans to protect themselves in a cold or hostile environment. This social network provided them with a sense of belonging that they could derive nowhere else."[11] To survive, many first-generation immigrants drew on their memories of cultural values to create new social structures that in turn became early expressions of Asian American identity.

A deep spiritual pain for Asian Americans today arises from the unresolvable conflict between the impossibility of letting go of one's own ethnic, cultural, and ancestral belonging and at the same time realizing that the assertion of one's own particularity is perceived as deviance by the society at large. "It wasn't until my mid-twenties that I even began to really appreciate my Filipino father and mother. . . . Sometimes, as I grew up, I was ashamed that my parents were Filipino with their accents and our home smelling 'funny' with the aroma of our ethnic food."[12] The ethnic and cultural distinctness of Filipino Americans is internalized by this second-generation Filipino as deviating from his perceived norm of the society.

A third-generation Japanese American reflects on the tension he experienced when having to choose between two cultural styles of dealing with his anger at the injustices endured in wartime by interned Japanese Americans. For him, as for many other Japanese Americans, life in America means embracing the unresolved conflict between their particularity and the ever-present forces that set them aside in the society: "The Asian in us tells us to feel shame and bear it and the American in us tells us to feel anger and to fight it. The dissonance can be emotionally painful, but fortunately most Asian Americans have learned from those who have preceded us to alternate bearing indignities with fighting back in the constant struggle to live in America." [13]

Yet there are others who attempt to "out-white the whites" in order to have their own place and being secured in this society. "Asian Americans born here are quite different from those who were born and raised in more homogeneous Asian environments (i.e., Japan, China, the Philippines, etc.). Many of us are very Westernized to the point of thinking and acting 'White.' We are educated with White American racist textbooks and at the same time are taught by our parents not to question authority." [14] An intentional obliteration of one's Asian Americanness is, however, inevitably met with the experience of their "deviant" status due to their "racial uniform" that can neither be discarded nor denied. "In White Suburbia, I led a sheltered life. My experiences were very middle class. Growing up in a white community made self-definition very difficult. With an Anglo norm, the Asian becomes the anomaly. Not quite fitting in makes one feel deviant. Self-hatred occasionally results from that," says a member of the Asian American Student Alliance at the University of California, Santa Cruz. [15] The late Joseph Kitagawa of University of Chicago observed that "many Asian-Americans, in their eagerness to be integrated into American society, often fall into the pitfall of considering the American heritage as simply an extension of Western (European) tradition in contradistinction to the Asian cultural traditions of their parents' original homelands. And they often overcompensate for their frustration of being discriminated against by identifying themselves, of all things, with a particular view of American culture as a transported form of a European paradigm."[16]

These experiences of Asian Americans are a yet another reminder of the deep pain of pluralism. To be an Asian American, no matter how the term is defined in today's ever-changing scene of ethnicity, is to live in the midst of a contradiction between the actualization of one's own ethno-cultural/social life and the thrust of the society toward a particular definition of universalism that excludes various subgroups. Thelma Adair, former moderator of Presbyterian Church U.S.A., echoes this dilemma. "Discussing the theme of 'Authenticity Before the Altar: Search for Community in the Midst of Denial, Betrayal, and Hope' is difficult because it causes us to look back, open old wounds, and be reminded again of the slow and tortuous trial of change."[17]

Asian Americans thus find ourselves in a state of liminality. The liminal person is one who has internalized the norms of a particular group but is not completely recognized by the members of that group as being a legitimate member. As long as this relationship prevails, one's role in countless situations will be ill-defined, or defined in different ways by the individual and the group as a whole. Such liminality leads to uncertainty, ambivalence, and the fear of rejection and failure. Sociologist Bok-Lim C. Kim argues that what is lacking in the school and home environment of Asian Americans is "a conscious articulation of the decisions, choices, and compromises" that need to be made in order to develop one's self.[18] Inevitably such decisions, choices, and compromises must be made. If not at home or at school, then at some point in the life of Asian Americans these decisions must be made in order to function as a member of society. Faith communities have been providing opportunities for this difficult but necessary grappling for identity.

Holy Insecurity

"The Cantonese have a word for Asians born in North America. The word is *jook sing.* It means empty bamboo. It also means something with no roots at either end. It is meant to be deroga-tory," says Kathryn Choy-Wong of American Baptist church.[19] This statement reflects the place of Asian Americans in this society. Asian Americans' search for identity has to do with the capacity to live in the midst of this unresolved and often contra-dictory and ambiguous state of life, in *jook sing*. The search for identity as reflected in Asian American communities of faith has more to do with the question of what it means to live a life that defies any attempt for a definition than with the question of who we are socially, psychologically, or even ethnically. The search for Asian American identity is also a quest for freedom to live in a world of ambiguity, in the midst of the "holy insecurity" of our liminal existence.

> *We Asians, as a whole, have worked hard in the United States. We've done so in the hopes of achieving a reasonable level of security. We've also discovered that diligence and hard work strike a harmonious chord with the best of the American spirit of industry and achievement. It is no small truism to say that the sojourner/stranger wants to be acceptable and secure in the land of which he is a part. The American notion of suc-cess and happiness has within it a passion to get rid of suffer-ing. However, as we would avoid suffering and pain, we discover that these are an integral part of life. The anguish of our living becomes more painful when we feel that our struggles and our suffering in life, the very existence which we endure, is meaningless.* [20]

This is the world of "holy insecurity" for Asian Americans.

To embrace the "holy insecurity" of a life, or being *jook sing*, that defies any conventional definition means to receive the gift of courage to live in the midst of an unresolved and often am-biguous state of life. It means to seek resources to function as human beings in the midst of the basic incompatibility between the ever-present reminders of the "racial uniform" we wear and the alienating universalism imposed by the dominant cultural group, and to do this without succumbing to its debilitatingly oppressive power. "Asian Americans' experiences are not just peripherality or liminality but rather forced, permanent, and comprehensive peripherality and forced, permanent, and comprehensive liminality. Empirically, they are marginal and not just peripheral or liminal," says Princeton theologian Sang Hyun Lee.[21]

The endeavor to live in a state of "forced liminality" is properly undertaken communally. Faith communities can provide such a setting. In Asian American churches, however, the ordering of life takes on a different expression from that of those who occupy the dominant power position in the society. In Asian American faith communities, "the salvation of the social disinherited," as H. Richard Niebuhr calls the life orientation of the marginalized, is indeed foundational to our collective identity and ordering of life. In other words, the ordering of life for Asian Americans, seen from the Christian faith perspective, is likely to focus on the needs of the disinherited and disfranchised in society, and it is suspicious of any assertion of power that denies the freedom of those with whom life is to be shared. The ordering of life in this fashion is likely to be expressed in terms of a shift in value orientation. Trust for the disfranchised, empathy for the disinherited, and dignity for the hopelessly uncredentialed are far more significant than certainty of a belief, consistency in logic, or even the hope for a progressively better future. The ordering of life revolves around these values that drive people to live.

The life of Grace United Methodist Church, a Filipino congregation in San Francisco, reveals its members' emerging collective identity as Filipino Americans. A majority of members are first- and second-generation Ilocanos, Tagalogs, and Visayans. There are also some surviving members of the former Parkside Methodist Church, which merged with Grace Church. The congregation is a center for these subgroups of Filipino ancestry. The church's excellent facilities—large fellowship hall and well-equipped kitchen—are available to all the church organizations and some community groups such as the Filipino Nurses' Association of San Francisco.

Social service is a particularly strong program of Grace Church. Noteworthy is the program for newly arrived Filipino immigrants. The program includes meeting them at the airport, locating housing and possibly employment, and placing their children in schools. Such socially extended ministries are repeated in other Filipino American congregations. Fred Ranches, pastor of a Filipino United Church of Christ congregation in Sunnyvale, California, comments: "We weren't welcome in many public places. So all the social affairs that you could go to are those that you'd have to plan yourself." Such endeavors are reminiscent of the "Daughters of the Philippines," which existed in the early days of Filipino American history. The "Daughters" consisted of twenty-five to thirty Filipino women who formed a community to engage in various social events and celebrations, particularly for single men, at a time when there were hardly any Filipino women around.

What the existence of these ministries of Asian American churches indicates is the intrinsically social and collective character of selfhood and the irreplaceable character of community for the well-being of Asian American Christians. Beverly Harrison and Carter Heyward talk about "self-integrity" and "other-integrity" rather than the notion of "the autonomy of identity" for women so that "we may simultaneously possess our own power, be empowered by others, and empower others. As rare as experiences of shared power are in this culture, it remains true that it is in these precious moments when isolation is broken that the possibility of community is grasped." [22] For Asian American Christians the social networks that are developed with our churches provide us with a sense of belonging and community that we could derive nowhere else. The primary concerns in these social networks of Asian American Christians are mutual recognition and shared power and not individuation in the form of differentiation. "It's with other Asian Americans, people at church, in my family and in the community that I reach towards for my individual and collective identity," says Henry Kim, associate pastor of Bethel Korean United Methodist Church in Santa Clara, California.

And yet the unresolved painful state of our culturally liminal lives continues to haunt us even in the midst of our efforts to challenge the perceived deviance of our beings by the society. The primary issue here is really spiritual in character, though it is expressed in the realm of culture and society. It is no longer adequate to talk about our identities just in terms of ethnicity and cultural and historical belonging. The quest for our identity cannot remain the narcissistic quest of an individual. The issues of identity for us are intrinsically human, communal, religious, and spiritual in character, encompassing the well-being of all people. These issues touch the very character of faith-understanding by Asian Americans. There are two other realms of Asian American liminality that need to be addressed: generational liminality and the place of Asian American women in society.

Inheritors of Pain: Generational Liminality

If deviance is the issue for the culturally liminal existence of Asian Americans, historically inflicted traumas impact the generationally liminal lives of Asian Americans. These traumas are the common thread that runs through the four ancestral groups of Asian American Christians. They create a significant difficulty in communication across the generations, often resulting in the alienation of younger generations from their parents' generations. These traumas also make the younger generation Asian Americans' role in the society uncertain and tenuous, and affect their identity concerns significantly. To a certain extent, the issues surrounding the generational differences and issues that arise out of them for Asian Americans are akin to what Robert Lifton terms the "marks of survival" of those who experienced historically inflicted trauma such as war.

During the early period of Korean American Christianity the churches were active in the Korean independence movement. The Korean independence movement (toward independence from the Japanese annexation of Korean following the Russo-Japanese War) united Korean Christians in North America. Some of these Christians benefited from the efforts of American missionaries in Korea to alleviate the suffering of people caught in the conflict. The second and third waves of Korean immigrants—those who immigrated in 1951–64 and following the Immigration and Naturalization Act of 1965—had gone through the trauma of World War II and particularly the Korean War. A substantial number of the North Korean refugees were Christians. Most established a new life in South Korea by starting small businesses, although a significant number entered professional fields later on. A survey in 1981 conducted by the Center for Asian American Ministries, School of Theology at Claremont, California, found that 22 percent of the Koreans in the Los Angeles area were born in North Korea. "This is in sharp contrast to the percentage of North Koreans in South Korea, where they comprise about 2 percent (675,000 persons) of the South Korean population."[23] These groups of people arrived at a time when ethnic and racial groups began to assert their identities and when there had been a shift in the American ethos away from monolithic assimilation and toward ethnic and cultural pluralism. The painful experiences of World War II and the Korean War and their impact on today's Korea serve as powerful undercurrents beneath these immigrants' assertion of their own places in this society.

While it is difficult to ascertain clearly the pattern of adjustment of these recent immigrant Koreans, sociologist Bok-Lim Kim argues that some features include (1) expectations of economic success in the majority culture, (2) retention of aspects of the Korean culture, (3) rapid flight to move to "desirable" housing in the suburbs, and (4) the development of ethnic business districts.[24] What is not mentioned in this list are the pervasive influences of the political situation of Korea on the Korean American community. Korean immigrants have shown a high degree of sensitivity and interest toward the affairs of their home country. Historically, this is reflected in the way the South Korean government has shown itself to be extremely sensitive to criticisms from domestic and overseas media, and has frequently used its power to control and censor information both inside and outside of Korea. The Korean-language press in America has been a target of such a control by the South Korean government.[25] Such a suppression of the Korean American media not only reflects a close connection between the life of Korean Americans and Korea but also points to the ways in which the aftermath of the Korean War still continues to affect the lives of Korean immigrants in America. Because of the high rate of North Korean immigrants among Christians, their ties with Korea, both North and South, do influence their relationship with the succeeding generations of Korean Americans who do not share to the same degree the painful experiences of their parents' historical past.

No doubt these factors are reflected in the life of Korean American churches. "The Korean churches are central to the Korean community," observe Harry Kitano and Roger Daniels, UCLA sociologists.[26] The church serves as a social and civic hub for their community. And yet these emerging patterns of Korean American community are not necessarily welcomed by what is now called the "one-point-five" generation of young Korean Americans, those who were born in Korea but mostly raised and educated in America. "I grew up attending a Korean church. We have a Korean household. I feel I lost out on American friends and culture. I play on the [men's] volleyball team at school, and I feel there is a distance between myself and the white players," comments Sang Shim, a University of Illinois junior.[27] In the face of phenomenal statistics on the number of Korean Americans who are involved in their churches, the presence of one-point-fives is startlingly limited. Of the Koreans who immigrated to the United States between 1974 and 1984, nearly 40 percent were people under the age of twenty.[28] A recent study found that 45.8 percent of those whose parents attend Korean immigrant churches will not attend Korean churches when they become adults, nor will they attend European American churches. The language differences between the generational groups contribute to the decline in church attendance. Most of the Korean American churches rely on the Korean language for communication. English-speaking Korean Americans often feel unaccepted by and alienated from the churches. Pastor K. Samuel Lee is critical of the Korean American churches: "[I]t is clear that most Korean-American churches have not been meeting the needs of the second generation Korean Americans."[29]

The detachment of the one-point-fives may have been due to the absence of children's and youth organizations within the immigrant churches. Or they might have been turned away by the constant in-fighting that takes place in church organizations. While it is inevitable that acculturation leads to conflict across generational differences, the absence of shared experience, particularly of the painful traumas of World War II, the Korean War, and the resulting state of Korea, accentuates generational alienation among Korean Americans. "As a minister for first generation Koreans, I tell people they should be ready for their death, in the sense that unless they die and are buried here, Koreans cannot claim the land," says Charles Ryu, pastor of Korean Methodist Church and Institute in New York City.[30] Sunny Kang, associate pastor of a suburban Glenview Korean Presbyterian Church near Chicago, and a one-point-five himself, points out the difficulty in empathizing with the people of his parents' generation who often seem preoccupied with death. "Why is it that people of my parents' generation are always talking so morbidly about death? Why their preoccupation with death? Is it because their experiences of the wars so impacted them that they have not been able to deal with the trauma of the war even today?"

The identity concerns of one-point-fives is not merely the matter of being caught between the dominant cultural values, such as individuality, autonomy, and competition, and their inherited Korean cultural values. They just do not have a clear understanding of the experiences of their parents' generation, particularly the traumatic and painful experience of living through two major wars. There is an unacknowledged legacy that they have to carry but did not live through. This results in an ambivalent relationship with the preceding generations of Korean immigrants, creating in the one-point-fives a sense of estrangement from both their Korean heritage and the mainstream U.S. culture. "I have an almost dual identity as a Korean Presbyterian, and at Northwestern there is not a large Korean community that can relate to this experience," says Arnold Park. The generational differences present an unresolved state of being for one-point-fives and subsequent generations.

The liminal nature of Asian American lives across generational lines is also the topic addressed by the Sansei Legacy Project initiated by Buena Vista United Methodist Church, a Japanese American congregation in Alameda, California. "Although most Sanseis were not alive during World War II, a growing number of us are discovering that our experiences of emotional, psychological, spiritual conflict or cultural discomfort seem to have significant roots in the internment camps—or more precisely, in the ways our Nisei parents reacted to the internment camps," says Jill Shiraki, a staff person for the project. "Our essential intent is to provide a forum whereby the 'wounds' of our past experiences as Japanese Americans can be understood and interpreted for the sake of our future as a people," states Michael Yoshii, pastor of the church.

Such concerns were initially voiced by Nobu Miyoshi, past director of family therapy at the University of Pennsylvania School of Medicine, a nisei who went through the internment experience herself. Miyoshi has sought to establish cultural ties to identity formation and bridge the communication breakdown between nisei parents and their sansei children. "An important objective in this type of family work is to ease relationships by encouraging dialogues among family members to bring to the surface protected, hidden and even unconscious loyalty obligations, myths and legends," says Miyoshi.[31] Issues surrounding the internment camps experiences of the issei and the nisei plague the sansei as they reach adolescence and beyond. The lack of communication regarding the camp experience between the sansei and the preceding generations is a symbol of intergenerational ethnic and personal alienation. What Miyoshi advocates and has attempted to create through the Sansei Legacy Project is open dialog across generational lines regarding the internment-camp experiences in order to address the sansei's identity concerns.

Sansei "seem to feel they are caught in a dilemma between their 'quiet' Nisei parents and their identity model of 'verbal'

Americans. Perhaps the seemingly passive attitudes of their parents concerning their camp experiences are symbolic of an identification barrier between the generations."[32] Nisei, on the other hand, are as a whole not consciously aware of their nonassertiveness even though they desire to become otherwise. "The Nisei's bland reactions to what is unmistakably a major personal and historical tragedy endured during the evacuation and incarceration highlights their deeply entrenched silence," observes Miyoshi.[33]

The reasons for the nisei's silence are manyfold: racial discrimination, their biculturality and defensive posture in the face of incarceration, nonverbal communication, and perhaps their inherited Japanese cultural values. In any case, the Nisei's silence and reticence to talk openly about their internment experiences result in the difficulty of cross-generational communication between them and their children. The sansei, whose lives have been extensively shaped by mainstream American cultural values as well as their acute political awareness growing out of events in recent American history, are puzzled as to the reason why their parents were silent and "weak" in exercising their rights as citizens of this nation.

The nisei, on the other hand, felt the need to face the pain of Pearl Harbor. They felt compelled to pay for the incident with suffering and sacrifice because of their Japanese blood and their internal conflict with their American heritage. "I see suffering of injuries sustained by the Nisei as loyalty payments and settlements to both heritages . . . [They] accepted the punishment by entering camp without disruptive protest."[34] The nisei's "payment" took its extreme form in the ultimate sacrifice of the celebrated all-nisei "suicide" battalion in the European Theater during World War II. "In an inexplicable spirit of atonement and with great sadness, we went with our parents to concentration camps," recalls one internee.[35]

The nisei's silence over their painful internment ordeal has become a serious obstacle to the succeeding generation's understanding. The difficulty in cross-generational communication is exacerbated by the nisei's desire to protect their children, to shield them from pain. They respond casually to their children's questions about the camps. "In their lives, the Sansei do not feel like they are assimilated Americans. They've been in white society and they discover that they have something else, the Japanese part in them," which has not been developed, in part because of their parents' silence about the camp experiences.

This unresolved pain suffered by the issei and the nisei generations has been passed down to the sansei generation through nonverbal cues that are particular to their cultural mode of communication. As a result, the sansei receive conflicting signals from their parents: "It's some sort of legacy we have to carry, but we didn't live through it . . . We're handed something we don't understand."[36] This in turn contributes to the sansei's ambiguity and discomfort within mainstream European American culture, sometimes resulting in a sense of estrangement from both their parents' generation and the dominant culture. They thus find themselves in an untenable liminal situation: "The Sansei receive strong, overt messages from their parents to become 'white,' i.e., to subscribe to the legacies of American society, almost exclusively. On the other hand, the sansei themselves are not only told by their major social environment that they are not white, but they themselves have yearnings for validation of their attitude and values that are unlike those encountered in their outside society," observes Miyoshi.[37] Unable to trust either their parents' cultural heritage or the dominant cultural traits of the society, the sansei find themselves in an untenable twilight zone of generational and cultural liminality not shared by others in this society. "The emotional insecurity of their American-born children . . . was chiefly caused by the citizen children's realization that they were self-consciously Americans, even though they were not warmly accepted by American society. At the same time, they were not understood by their parents, and they were not basically at home in the racially segregated communities," observes Joseph Kitagawa.[38] The trauma of the nisei generation is passed on to the sansei in this fashion.

There are other historical incidents of inflicted trauma that present disturbing legacies to succeeding generations. Yale psychologist Robert Lifton has coined the term "psychic numb-ing" to describe the overwhelming intensity of the impact of a trauma upon the survivors. It is the psychic closing off, or numb-ing, of a survivor in response to an unbearable experience. The setting for Lifton's research is Hiroshima.[39] "Psychic numbing" is one of the characteristics of those who survive an cataclysmic event, along with the death imprint, death guilt, conflicts around nurturing and contagion, and struggles with meaning or formula-tion.[40] Lifton suggests that the survivors of Hiroshima (the *Hiba-kusha*) either affirm life or subvert it. They develop the polarity of "reintegration versus residual mistrust."[41] In either case, they have to live with the unresolved meaning of their experiences of the trauma.

Florence Date Smith could not bring herself to talk about her internment experience for thirty-five years. "I know now that it would have been healthy to talk and that I should have done it thirty or forty years ago. But we were such zombies then. We thought it was violent or disrespectful to react like that. The experience was too traumatic; it devastated our personhood. This happened to all of us."[42] The long process of "reintegration" just recently began for Date Smith. However, it is not up to the nisei parents alone to explain or describe the implications of their experiences. It is "a joint venture wherein parents and their children assist each other to listen, to confidently ask difficult questions, and to gain the courage necessary to confront the pain, the shame, as well as the poignant and pleasurable mo-ments associated with incarceration," says Nobu Miyoshi.[43]

The Sansei Legacy Project began as a witness of Buena Vista United Methodist Church through a community self-determination grant from the United Methodist Commission on Religion and Race. Is it really a coincidence that the Christian faith community came to recognize the significance of the legacy of the internment experience upon the new generations of Japa-nese Americans and has decided to take on the challenge of facing up to it? The Christian faith as lived within the faith community of Japanese Americans has developed a degree of sensitivity to the pain and suffering that are imposed unjustly upon them from outside. The message of the "officially optimistic faith," as theologian John Douglas Hall describes the dominant American Christian tradition, is not readily present in Japanese American faith reflections. "'Heart Mountain' is a strange name, but those who spent a few years there will never forget the name. For it was a place of human struggle and pain. But, God was present in the midst of their suffering. . . . [T]he undying faith which is symbolized in the Cross . . . towered over the camp. This faith kept the people together as a loving community in the midst of agony. 'No, in all these things we have complete victory through him who loves us.' (Rom. 8:37)"[44] The faith community serves as a place where the impact of historically inflicted injuries can be faced and coped with by Asian Americans.

A Double Bind: Women in Church

Historical inflicted trauma has a different but no less acute and tenacious effect on Asian American women, both within the very structure of our society and in the cultural legacy carried over from Asia. "I am the double minority, the double marginalized, the confused, 'the other,' and 'the et cetera,'" laments Soomee Kim Hwang, a former seminary student at the School of Theology at Claremont.[45] "Take away the race issue and they remain women. Take away the gender issue and they remain persons of color."[46] This mixture of culture and gender presents a distinct liminal experience for Kim Hwang and others like her. Questioned about her cultural/ethnic and gender identity, she replied: "[I]f I want to be true to myself, I have to be a woman first. I hope people don't see my black hair and brown eyes before they see a woman."[47]

To be a woman within the Asian American community is an experience that artist-scholar Janice Tanaka and other Asian American women call the "double bind." In addition to being a member of a marginal Asian American subculture that functions with rules the majority does not live by, women often experience the frustration of not having their experiences recognized, validated, and supported by men within their own ethnic community. This double bind points to the way matters of gender and race intersect with each other. In wider society, Asian American women are subject to both racism against people of color and sexism against women. At the same time, they are also subjected to the sexism stemming from the legacy of Confucian patriarchy within the Asian American community. Living with this double bind as a double minority results in the liminal status of Asian American women that is being addressed in the faith community.

A particular difficulty Asian American women face is that of their social status being defined in relation to the family and also in relation to men. In the Asian American community, family responsibilities continue to be strongly emphasized, particularly for women. In a survey of over six hundred Chinese American, Filipino American, Japanese American, and Korean American middle school, high school, and college women conducted in 1980–81 in the San Francisco Bay Area, Pauline Fong found that the vast majority wanted to be wives and mothers. There was an intense interest in work as a contribution to family life. "Family is why you work," according to one respondent.[48] This situation seems to be conditioned by the Confucian patriarchy that continues to exist within Asian American communities, particularly within the East Asian American setting. "Institutional inequality is built into the Confucian system, which defines a person's status, role, privileges, duties, and liabilities within the family and social order according to age, class, and gender."[49] In the traditional Confucian worldview, women are excluded from the public sphere. Motherhood is regarded as a woman's proper avenue to security, respect, and power.

Within the faith community such a definition of Asian American women is supported by the fact that motherhood is considered a primary role of women. "But it comes into conflict with women who are ordained, even though some of us are married and there are some clergy that are mothers. Still there's that image of the person in robes being an authority up there is not the image of themselves that they perceive."[50] This is a problem facing not only Asian American women pastors, but also other active lay women in the church, who are often rele-gated to the nursery or children's classes rather than being given leadership roles. This perception is reinforced within Asian American churches because they are "mostly still immigrant churches, and they tend to be preservers of the culture back in Asia."[51]

But, Elaine Kim cautions, "Although sexism has been an issue in Asian American communities, racism has usually been pinpointed as the more important barrier to social and economic equality for Asian American women."[52] In America today, rac-ism and sexism work together to create a hierarchy of domina-tion that places European American males on top and women of color at the bottom. "Unavoidably, patriarchy American style shapes Asian American women's lives, I think, to a greater de-gree now than the Confucian variety that shapes the lives of our sisters in Asia," Kim points out.[53] In America's patriarchal sys-tem women's sexuality is reified and commodified. This is partic-ularly the case for Asian American women. A woman's worth is often measured according to her appearance, her physical attrac-tiveness to men. This is the real expression of American racism, in the form of sexism. "The popular image of Asian women as obedient, eager to please, and simple to satisfy makes it all the more difficult for us to overcome race and sex discrimination," says Greer Ann Ng, who is on the faculty at Vancouver School of Theology.

How are Asian American women, particularly within the faith community, responding to this societally and culturally im-posed racism and sexism? "If we are going to be serious about how to proceed from this point in history into the future while em-bracing our Christian values of equality and justice, we are going to have to take the time to reassess, to rebuild, to refocus and to initiate a new vision which, once again, champions the cause of our women, our children, and our sisters and brothers," says Diana Akiyama, assistant dean at the Stanford Memorial Church and the first Japanese American woman to be ordained into the Episcopal priesthood.[54] Elaine Kim echoes Akiyama's vision: "We must shape a new context, a context that does not polarize male and female but allows us to exist on a continuum. . . . [W]e need solidarity with one another as we begin our efforts to claim our place in human history, to transform our communities, and define ourselves."[55]

Such a new definition by Asian American women goes on within the liminal existence of their "double bind" and "double minority." Janice Tanaka is acutely aware of the liminal state of Asian American women. In "Memories from the Department of Amnesia," a documentary about the death of her mother, she faces the unresolved pain of being an Asian American woman whose attempts at balance and security were constantly disrupted by social, cultural, political, and personal forces beyond her control. The video project is her process of grieving, of dealing with the way in which memory operates and the emotions memory arouses. When Tanaka was asked if the project was very healing, she responded: "I don't like the word 'healing' because it seems to imply there's something wrong with the person who is feeling the impact of an experience. And too, the word implies a finalization when the feeling never stops, it never goes away. One has a broader understanding of that experience."[56]

Soomee Kim Hwang describes her experience of being a "double minority": "I thank God for the difficulties I had searching for my true identity. I thank God for making the rainbow, the rainbow with beautiful primary colors and lots of in-between colors. When we mix red and yellow, we have orange. . . . Yet orange is not red, orange is not yellow. Orange is another color with its own name and its own color. . . . I am a one-point-five generation Korean American woman. I thank God I am the 'in-between.' In-between colors have names, too."[57]

Theologian Rita Nakashima Brock identifies three aspects of what she terms "the hermeneutics of wisdom" to articulate the state of Asian American women: "(1) how the past retains meaning for the present at the same time that the Confucian patriarchal tradition loses its authoritative status; and (2) how innocence is understood as something that must be outgrown . . . ; (3) the maturation of wisdom, through which life is maintained and passed on through generations." She makes this identification by reflecting on two stories by Asian American women, Wendy Law-Yone's *The Coffin Tree* and Amy Tan's *The Joy Luck Club*. What Nakashima Brock strives for is "a tribal consciousness," an awareness of the many complex aspects of Asian American women's identity.[58] Her vision is that "to be less polemical and more nuanced in our thinking about innocence, oppression, and justice may help take us past the deadlock of self-righteousness, defensiveness, and a compensatory understanding of diversity and help us toward relationship that creates a diverse community."[59]

Promise in Pain

We have seen the fluid and complex nature of Asian American Christians' search for an identity, often fraught with unresolved pain. What this indicates is the fundamentally ambiguous and yet dynamic ordering of life. This ordering suspects the particular socially constructed actuality of the society which values those who are in the position of dominance and control. The ordering of life in this fashion, moreover, is likely to be expressed in terms of a shift in value orientation. Hospitality for the stranger, empathy for the disfranchised, and courage to face the future, even amidst an overwhelmingly adverse condition, are far more significant than correct doctrine and consistency in logic. It is, in fact, the experience and acceptance of an ambiguous and dynamic state of life that allows a person the transformation of values and worldviews. "A prominent theme in the comments by Korean American students was: 'We are here to stay!' This statement is both a recognition and an affirmation. This statement is recognizing that the second generation Korean Americans do not feel at home in America which is where they are born and which is the only place that can be their home. This statement is also an affirmation that no one can deny this country's someday becoming their true home."[60] Identifying himself as an American, but rejected because of his Asian ancestry, Ken Kitagawa, a nisei, searched for an intellectual resolution to his liminality. "I thought of myself, racially a child of the Orient, culturally a child of the Occident, embodying within me the clash and the adjustment and the synthesis of the East and the West, a microcosm reflecting the macrocosm of the world problem of race and culture; I am both East and West made into one whole. I had at last found my field. The peculiar work for which I had been ordained was to be just myself; my very self as an interpretation of the East and West; my life work would be that of an interpreter of the East to the West and of the West to the East."[61] Kitagawa no longer felt compelled to be a poor imitation of either an American or a Japanese. He could be "authentic" without facing the disappointments he had previously experienced when "excluded from either side." By reidentifying his position, he sought to establish a new stance that addressed his liminal world: the acceptance of and embracing of the liminal state of life, the place of the "holy insecurity," indeed the home for Asian Americans.

Such a transformation of worldviews and value assumptions, furthermore, is not confined merely to the personal dimension. It takes place also at the societal level. Those who exist in a world of liminality are apt to recognize that the present world is indeed a socially constructed system and therefore one does not necessarily have to be bound by its stated or unstated rules. The ordering of life that is born out of the deep pain of incompatibility in this society enables one to see the world for what it really is. Occupying an insignificant place in the society, being a "minor key," makes one much more attuned to the subversive vision in the gospel, which reveals a world whose emperors have no clothes save those tailored by their own ostentatious claims to power and privilege, bolstered by their conspicuous consumption.

The thematic universe (world) shaped by the power of assimilation and inclusion into the dominant world, even with its enormously powerful claim to this society, is indeed a limited situation that does not always have to be a fixed and closed system. The inability to relate across generational lines because of the lack of a shared experience of trauma does not need to set the tone for the probing of identity for a new generation of people. The racism and sexism woven into the very fabric of our society need not be legitimized and accepted. To be sure, the existing orderings of life in this society are not about to be replaced any time soon. Nor is any blueprint for the future available. The liminal state of Asian American lives does not provide any easy resolution. The truth is that our unresolved state of liminality has a variety of expressions. As Tanaka points out, there is no "healing" in such a state "because it seems to imply there's something wrong with the person who is feeling the impact of an experience." What is needed is a courage and resolution to live in the midst of the unresolved and often ambiguous state of being. Then "one has a broader understanding of that experience."

The capacity to live the life of ambiguity, or the "courage to be," is not merely the capacity to endure the status quo, however. It is, instead, the freedom to live in a world of pain without being complacent about and acquiescing to its own ordering power. It is the freedom to shatter the complacency of the existing order without even a blueprint for what the world beyond it looks like. Such a freedom, by nature, transcends the existing situation or conceptual ideal. It breaks into the world from beyond. It exists in the realm of faith. And it takes a certain social, cultural, ethnic, or class location in which one exists, a place of the "holy insecurity," a fringe, to become receptive to such a freedom, a promise given in the good news. "Once we begin to look to this relationship to the Ultimate Power, and rearrange our personal and social relationships to that power, we discover tremendous possibilities open to us. We are introduced to real freedom."[62]

In a culture that tempts us with wishful optimism, the Christian faith is also afflicted with the ordering of life—of equilibrium, coherence, and the assumed sense of symmetry. Asian American experiences of liminality defy such a perspective. Life is savagely marked by disequilibrium, dissolution, and unrelieved asymmetry. Our faith experience cannot ignore this reality. "In my sermons, I talk about immigration theology. We would liken our experiences to what happened to Abraham and the wandering tribes. It is a way to incorporate our alien status in this country, to justify our existence and why we are here," says

Wontae Chu, senior pastor of Korean Methodist Church and Institute in New York City.[63] When a sermon of hopeful future is preached in an Asian American church, what it signals is not so much a validation of an "officially optimistic" society but a form of defiance in which order and reliability are flung in the face of disorder and ambiguity. "Why did we not lose heart and escape into an immobilized life of resentment and cynicism? Why are we able to maintain a sane view of ourselves, with a sense of humor, waiting patiently for the day of vindication? Because Jesus Christ rescued and delivered us out of our feelings of futility," Baptist pastor Jitsuo Morikawa once proclaimed from the pulpit.[64] In this way, we insist that nothing shall separate us from the love of God. Such an incongruity between our life experience of disorder and our "faith speech" of coherence of life is a faith expression of "nevertheless" (Heb. 3:18). Such a counterstatement insists that life has its own integrity even in the midst of its unresolved state. Stories of faith speak truly, even if the world is experienced otherwise.

But this is only partly true. The reality is that the faith experiences of Asian American Christians are also conditioned by the prevailing optimism of the dominant culture; by a frightened, numb denial and deception that do not want to acknowledge or experience the ambiguous and unresolved state of life. And yet the painful reality breaks in at times to remind us of the unsatisfactoriness of a mere optimistic response in the face of our liminal existence with its disequilibrium, dissolution, and asymmetry. The unresolved state of life we notice in faith may be judged by the world to be failure, if not an act of unfaith. But for the trusting community, it is an act of bold faith, albeit a transformed faith. It is an act of bold faith, on the one hand, because it insists that the world must be experienced as it really is and not in some pretended way. On the other hand, it is bold because it insists that all such experiences of disorder and ambiguity are a proper subject for discourse with God. Proclaimed Jitsuo Morikawa:

> Tonight we are engaging in a celebration, in remembrance of the God of Exodus, Christ of the Cross and Resurrection,

> *Who has wrought a mighty redemption, delivered us from the bondage of despair and self-rejection to a life of meaning, dignity and pride. When the real history of America is written, one of the incredible high points—a miracle of history—will be the story of the Japanese Americans. By every measure of social analysis they should be a broken, defeated, decimated people, a tragic casualty on the junk-heap of history. . . . Nevertheless, they refused to give up . . . Japanese-Americans today occupy positions of trust and responsibility in the most sensitive areas of our national life. . . . This miracle of history has been wrought by the One "Who has put down the mighty from their thrones and exalted those of low degree."* [65]

There is nothing out of bounds, nothing precluded or inappropriate. To withhold parts of life from that conversation is in fact to withhold part of life from the sovereignty of God. Faith experiences of Asian Americans insist that everything must be brought to speech, often in resolute defiance of the hostile world around us. Everything brought to speech must be addressed to God in trust, who is the final reference of all life.

Such a faith is indeed a transformed faith, one that does not conform. The community that uses these speeches is not easily linked with the prevailing optimistic faith of the society, which goes "from strength to strength." It is, rather, faith in a very different God, one who is present in, participating in, and attentive to disequilibrium, liminality, and asymmetry. "Even in Poston and Manzanar and Gila Rivers we did not lose our dignity and vision of hope . . . at this moment in our wilderness history we must surely pause and reflect over our ninety-five years of magnificent history, and offer thanks for the wondrous deed of God that he delivered us out of despair and hopelessness and discouragement into a life of hope and patient endurance, expectancy and achievement, which transformed suffering into creative activity."[66] The God assumed and addressed is a God "of sorrows, and acquainted with grief." It is more appropriate to speak to this God in the categories of fidelity than of immutability, and when fidelity displaces immutability, our notion of God's sovereignty is deeply changed.

But the transformation concerns not only God. Life also is transformed. Now life is understood to be a pilgrimage or journey through the darkness that belongs properly to humanness. While none would choose to be there, such seasons of life are not always experiences of failure for which guilt is to be assigned. They may be a placement in life for which the human person or community is not responsible and therefore not blamed. Precisely in such painful and often hopeless situation as presented in our life experiences is an opportunity for the "in-breaking" of newness in life. We do not understand how that could be so or even why it is so. But we regularly learn and discern that there—more than anywhere else—newness that is not of our own making breaks in such a moment. "We still are a pursuing church, or the pilgrim of God in the wilderness. . . . [W]e are all on the way, together. But we are not alone, nor helpless. Our fathers crossed over the Pacific for a new life in this land. They found what the life of sojourners was like, and yet, wherever they were, they were not away from the Lord's field. They met him, and built their churches."[67] Reinhold Niebuhr coined the term "indefinite transcendence." What Niebuhr means by this term is that all persons have only partial control over the circumstances of their lives, never fully escaping the limitations and prejudices that mark their starting points, but never simply bound to those limitations either. That capacity for self-transcendence makes possible all our illusions, but it is also the source of our freedom and creativity.

The linguistic function here is that our speech may hopefully evoke reality for someone who has engaged in self-deception and still imagines and pretends that life is well ordered, when in fact it is not. The denial may be of a broken relationship. "I have been much disheartened by Asian American men's unwillingness to challenge either the Asian American patriarchy and the American racist variety. Many of our most progressive thinkers have relegated women's issues to the domain of family and personal life, outside the larger aegis of the political economy, thereby rendering themselves immune to feminist challenges."[68] The harsh and abrasive language of disequilibrium may penetrate the deception and lead us to reality. In such a case, language leads to experience, so that what the speaker speaks is unknown and unexperienced until it is actually brought to speech. In other words, it is not this way until it is said to be this way. Women in Asian American churches are apt to take on this prophetic function.

It is no wonder that our society has intuitively avoided the churches that have taken on such a challenge. Those churches lead us into dangerous acknowledgment of how life really is. They lead us into the presence of God where everything is not polite and civil. They cause us to think unthinkable thoughts and utter unutterable words. Perhaps worst, they lead us away from the comfortable religious claims prevalent in our modern society in which everything is managed and controlled. In our modern experience, but probably also in every successful and affluent culture, it is believed that enough power and knowledge can tame the terror and eliminate pain. But our Asian American experience, both personal and public, attests to the resilience of the counterforces, in spite of us. The remarkable thing about faith is that it does not banish or deny the forces from its religious enterprise. It embraces them as the very stuff of new life. Indeed, faith community seems to know that new life comes nowhere else.

Whether such speech articulates, illuminates, or evokes experience, it does move the awareness and imagination of the speaker away from well-ordered life into an arena of terror, raggedness, and hurt. In some sense this speech is a visceral release of the realities and imagination that have been censored, denied, or held in check by the dominant claims of society. For that reason, it does not surprise us that sermons preached in Asian American churches tend toward hyperbole, vivid imagery, and statements that offend "proper" and civil religious sensitivities.

> [O]ur parents, out of their weakness and meagerness, ministered generously to the weak. We are called to act out of our abundance and power not only to the weak, but to face and confront and challenge the powerful of this world. We have

> *fresh in our memories what powerful forces in American cul-*
> *ture have done to us. Presidents, Congress, Supreme Court,*
> *mass media, local governments, economic interests, conspired*
> *together to defraud and to deprive and to rob us of our free-*
> *dom; and we must now . . . not betray our fellow men who*
> *are now suffering by accommodation, capitulation and moral*
> *surrender to the powerful . . .* [69]

These sermons are a means of expression that tries to match experience, that also does not fit with the accepted and acceptable religious sensitivity. That is, in "proper" religion such an expression should not be expressed. What is implicit in the proper order is also that these experiences should not be experienced. They are speech "at the limit," speaking about experience "at the limit" in the dominant order of life.

≈≈ 3

A Stone That Cries Out
An Alternative Understanding of Community Amidst a Racist Society

Does "claiming America" mean assimilation of American values? No. I mean it as a response to the legislation and racism that says we of Chinese origin do not belong here in America. It's a response to the assumption that I come from Vietnam or another Asian country. When I say that I am a native American with all the rights of an American, I am saying, "No, we're not outsiders; we Chinese belong here. This is our country, this is our history, we are a part of America. If it weren't for us, America would be a different place." [1]

Why is it that what seems to be an obvious fact—Asian Americans' claims to our American identity and distinct personhood— cannot be easily acknowledged in this society? Why do Asian Americans continue to experience the societal confusion of our national identity? It stems to a large extent from the entrenched racism in American society, which enhances the well-being of certain members at the expense of the impoverishment of others. Racism is oppressive not because people of a dominant group have prejudicial feelings about others, but because it is a system that promotes the domination and subjugation of certain racial and ethnic groups. It is the intentional or unintentional use of power on the part of those who are in the position of power culturally, politically, and economically to isolate, separate, and exploit those who are less powerful and vulnerable. Racism is enforced and maintained by the legal, cultural, religious, educational, economic, political, and military institutions of a society. The confusion between Americans of Asian descent and Asian nationals stems not merely from the racial and physiological characteristics that we share. The primary cause is that the ethnic and cultural distinctness of those who fall outside the dominant group norm in this society is relativized and trivialized in order to maintain the legitimacy of the dominant cultural norm. The relativization takes place, furthermore, because North American society is binarily differentiated between a norm-producing group and the rest. This differentiation is structured as diametrically opposite through political, linguistic, cultural, and subjective practices.[2] Social, cultural, and political manifestations of Asian American separatism are often perceived as a sign of "anti-American" movement in this society when they usually represent an attempt by Asian Americans to construct places of political and cultural sanctuary where we can "be ourselves" among a variety of groups.

When a person does not fit into the accepted norm of society because of the perceived peculiarity of that person's racial or ethnic uniform, then that person is not likely to be acknowledged as a member in this society and is apt to be categorized as a foreigner, an alien, or worse, anti-American. "The view, a very powerful view, is that American means European ancestry, American means white," says Ronald Takaki. "Christian churches in America, for the most part, shared the indifference of the general public, in fact, some ardent church members on the West Coast were also noted for their anti-Asiatic campaigns," particularly during World War II, observes Joseph Kitagawa.[3] Christian churches are by no means exempted from the binarily differentiated structure of the American society in which they exist. They are very much embedded in the prevailing dominant culture and are shaped by it.

History reveals that personal identity in America is understood primarily in terms of dichotomy and opposition of others. It is historically based on first the exclusion and then the subjugation of other groups by the norm-setting group. To "admit foreigners indiscriminately to the rights of citizens, the moment they put foot in our country . . . would be nothing less than to admit the Grecian horse into the citadel of our liberty and sovereignty," wrote Alexander Hamilton in 1802. In the latter part of the nineteenth century, when the "middle class" began to emerge as a dominant cultural force among the European American population, its identity as both exclusive and dominant over others was expressed in terms of a "calculating effort to move up the ladder of success," says Robert Bellah.[4] The status mobility of the European American middle class could not be easily achieved without a further domination and subjugation of those who were economically, politically, and racially "deviating" from the prevailing cultural norm. "It is the middle-class orientation toward technical education, bureaucratic occupational hierarchies, and the market economy that encourages the greater emphasis on universal rules and technical rationality."[5] European American Protestant leadership in America also contributed to the status mobility, argues William Greenbaum of Harvard. "The quintessence of Protestant leadership in America has been distance from other people. This propensity to distance, with its tendency to rationalize human existence, was inherited from Western and Northern European traditions; it lay at the root of the Protestants' ability to build an allegedly impersonal, bureaucratic, capitalist order, and, at the same time, it was the source of their special ability to regard people as commodities."[6] The domination and subjugation of people of color and others who "deviate" from the middle-class norm was accomplished by creating a societal structure disposed favorably to the worldview and cultural values of the dominant group. This has become the foundation of American racism.

In such a setting the search for human identity tends to become individualistic and introspective rather than collective and relation-oriented. Personhood is defined largely in terms of one's autonomous existence, differentiation, and binary opposition. The Cartesian notion of human self does undergird this basic orientation and outlook of life. However, there are other factors as well that have contributed to this orientation. Sociologists David Schneider and Raymond Smith see the individual and social behavior of the European American middle class as "predominantly determined by the application of technical rules to any situation that arises."[7] The culture of technical and bureaucratic rationality reflects its assumptive worldview of autonomy and separation. Interestingly enough, however, both lower- and upper-class European Americans have a more "dramaturgical view of social action that takes on meaning because of a particular history of relationships. . . . [I]t is in the lower class that ethnicity, as a specific pattern of cultural life, survives in America, and that as individuals enter the middle class, ethnicity loses distinctive social content even when it is symbolically emphasized."[8]

The dominance of the middle-class cultural ethos in society, however, accentuates individual autonomy as the primary concern of human identity and relegates the distinctness of ethnic and cultural characteristics to marginality. The racial uniform of Asian Americans is a deviation from the predominant norm and is associated with alien and therefore strange cultures. When personhood is defined in association with race and its correlative culture, then it is likely to be perceived as an anomaly to be treated as inconsequential to the autonomy-based definition of personhood. "I was most recently a member of a presbytery in which one other Asian American was a member; and there were presbyters in that presbytery who never ceased to confuse the two of us (although there were no physical resemblances apart from the fact that we both were Asian Americans)," says Frank Ichishita, one-time Associate for Asian Mission Development of the Presbyterian Church U.S.A.[9] Any alternative definition of personhood or identity is discriminated against and is necessarily excluded from consideration in order to maintain the domination of a particular cultural and ethnic group.

Thus our society's inclination toward atomic individualism

is by no means isolated from the reality of Asian Americans' experiences of racism. Asian Americans see racism as having been internalized and institutionalized to the point of being an essential and inherently functioning component of this society. Racism is a powerful expression of the prevailing dominant culture and is designed to enhance the well-being and survival of certain members of society by marginalizing the personhood, worldviews, and cultural values of others. Racism against Asian Americans "is not a new phenomenon and should not be viewed as a temporary aberration in American society. Rather, there has been, and continues to be, an ongoing complex relationship between Asian immigration, American cultural self-perception, American domestic and foreign policies, American political economy, and American racism," points out Presbyterian Wesley Woo.[10] From the time of the founding of American society, racial discrimination has been a regulative force for maintaining stability and growth and for maximizing cultural values of certain segments of people, particularly those who are in the position of dominance, at the expense of others. No wonder the predominant literature on the subject of human identity and personhood in the European American culture, written primarily by its male members, is based on the restrictive assumption of the individuation and autonomy of people, disallowing the emergence of alternative views until quite recently.

Asian American lives are rooted intimately in the distinct characteristics of our ethnic groupings and our cultural heritages. Our primary identity concerns arise less from the question of who we are as individual persons; our sense of personal identity is primarily embedded in specific patterns of relationship and solidarity that mitigate the tendency toward a preoccupation with self and overly utilitarian relationships. This is not necessarily inherited from our Asian cultural heritages as popularly assumed. It is indeed necessary for us to "stay together" in the often hostile environment of the American society. Calvin Chin, a Presbyterian pastor in San Francisco's Chinatown, recalls how Chinatowns were developed as a necessary refuge, perhaps the only available haven for Chinese Americans: "The Chinese survived by resorting to the same survival mechanism of their peasant cultural psychology, 'take care of your own.' We dignified our withdrawal into our Chinatowns by taking care of our own, minding our own business, staying to ourselves, avoiding conflict and controversy." [11]

This communal pattern of life is a necessary defense in a inhospitable and racist society. Asian American Christians are particularly concerned about the uncritical equation of faith with the underlying individualism of the prevailing dominant culture. Presbyterian Wesley Woo says that we

> ask if being Christian requires, or necessarily results in, a loss of Asian or Asian American identity and their resultant dislocation and alienation from Asian American communities. [We] are troubled by the generally facile confoundation of Christianity and American and European culture. After all, Protestantism has been at the core of American culture and perhaps its key shaping force—in positive and negative ways. At times it seems impossible to be Christian without being Americanized and "Anglo-cized." [12]

Asian American Christians are troubled by such an equation of Christian faith and a particular culture precisely because it reinforces the fundamental racist orientation of this society, which keeps us in a vulnerable and unprotected state. The issue of Christ and cultures is not of mere academic concern for Asian American Christians. It is fundamentally an issue of survival in a hostile environment.

As Asian Americans grapple for identity, we are constantly reminded that we are an insignificant people, a minor key, in this society. Issues of ethnically based identity continue to be a primary concern among Asian Americans and will remain a major theme in our theological thought as long as the forces of cultural alienation and oppressive racism in American society persist. Must we couch our search for identity in terms of the clinical language of psychology and therapy that have been shaped in post-Enlightenment Europe and America? To do so would vali-

date the unstated assumptive worldview of the European American middle-class orientation toward technical education, bureaucratic occupational hierarchies, and the market economy that
encourages the greater emphasis on technical rationality, individuation, and autonomy.

It is more appropriate for us to pose the question of identity
honestly within the specificity of our concrete Asian American
experiences so that an uncritical acquiescence to racism can be
avoided. "The principal intent is for us to reflect on our experiences in such a way that we may come to understand God's
relationship with us in leading us to where we are now. In one
sense, we are ethnic peoples who look at our role and place in
this land from the perspective of our ethnic heritage. However,
when we go deeper into this study, we find that we do not remain
merely ethnic peoples. We join our humanity along with other
human beings." [13] As stated in chapter 1, race and ethnicity are
not entirely inherent or natural traits, although physical characteristics certainly have a lot to do with how people categorize
members of racial and ethnic groups. What is at stake is that
racial and ethnic identities derive their meanings from social and
historical circumstances and that these identities can vary over
time. What is at stake theologically is the created order of the
just relatedness of all people including the distinctness of each
person, amidst the painful reality of the estrangement of one
group from another. Theologically the issue is also witnessing to
the promise of reconciled relationships among people of all color
within the historical context of imposed pain that people of color
have been experiencing in North American society.

In other words, in North America, personhood needs to be
understood theologically in terms of the actuality of alienation in
our racist society and the potential for reconciled interaction and
interdependence. Given the atomized individualism that shapes
the American societal ethos, how do Asian Americans grapple
with what Karl Barth calls "the basic form of humanity," the
reality of humanity as encountered and in relationship with
others? The question is necessarily theological. The issue cannot
be stated otherwise: If the basic relational form of humanity is in

trouble, the gospel is in jeopardy. Barth knew this to be so in the context of the German nightmare in the tempestuous decades of the 1930s and 1940s. Asian American Christians know this same meaning in the context of our struggle with racism. In U.S. society, Martin Luther King, Jr., for one, articulated his vision for humanity as a beloved community where all people have value in and of themselves and are subjects worthy of love. He took on the redemption of a society divided by the excess of extraordinary racial privilege on the one hand and the persistent challenge of racial conventions on the other. He challenged Americans to lay full claim to the basic relational form of humanity. Theologically central issues here are the possibilities and limits of a shared future mutuality witnessed by our ecclesial communities in the midst of the actuality of racism experienced by Asian Americans and other American racial and ethnic groups. Ethnically segregated churches are a place of opportunity for resistance and reconciliation and mutuality. They are the place where the vision of mutual relatedness can be embodied. The issue here is not just that of critiquing the status quo. It is about transforming the image, creating an alternative social order, asking ourselves questions about the types of images that subvert, posing critical alternatives, and transforming our worldviews, moving us away from dualistic, bipolar thinking about humanity. When the historical victims of racism, silenced people, find their voices and begin to speak for themselves, new interpretations of Christian symbols emerge, as do new analyses of social structures, critiques of the institutional structure of the church, and solidarity with those who are in a similar circumstance.

Racism and an Alternative Vision of Personhood/Peoplehood

That questions are raised in some quarters about Americans' preoccupation with ethnicity and culture is indicative of the fact that American society has not created alternatives for the rich cultures and ethnic communities that Americans identify with our immigrant parents and grandparents. This explains in part why people of color often cling to ethnic distinctness and why they crave ritual and a sense of belonging. But can ethnicity, especially in its attenuated forms, provide the nexus for social life that it did in another era for people quite unlike ourselves? Can it be more than a palliative for spiritual yearnings that are not fulfilled elsewhere? The ultimate myth surrounding ethnicity, perhaps, is the belief that the cultural symbols of the past can provide more than a comfortable illusion to shield us from present-day discontents. The central problems for Asian Americans have to do, ultimately, not with ethnic groupings or the distinctness of our cultural heritages as such, but with racism and its manifestations in American economic policy, social rule, and class relations that, in devaluing our ethnic and cultural characteristics, alienate us from other members of the society. We must address the reality, as Derick Bell forcefully argues, that we live in a society in which racism has been internalized and institutionalized to the point of being an essential and inherently functioning component of that society—a culture from whose inception racial discrimination has been a regulative force for maintaining stability and growth.

From the perspective of many Asian American Christians' faith-understanding, the most basic form of humanity is "humanity-in-encounter." Personhood cannot be separated from peoplehood. "The sacred bond that Asian American people have cultivated transmits all theologies. The main question to answer therefore is, 'How do we foster this sacred bond? . . . The sacred bond is going to have to transcend dogmatism, parochialism, nationalism, and language," says Jeff Murakami of the University of Southern California, a member of the United Church of Christ.[14] The phrase "I am" is to be taken to mean "I am-in-encounter," or, in the words of Barth, "I am as Thou art." The meaningfulness of life derives from engagement and commitment to this fundamental reality of humanity which is the "sacred bond," or "chains of promise of mutuality and interdependence" as the late Baptist pastor Jitsuo Morikawa puts it. Racism counters this basic expression of humanity and undermines the very coherence of human relatedness. It is a theological concern precisely because racism challenges the visible integrity of the basic form of humanity that is expressed in the revelatory presence of the one Christ in the midst of human community, by which life is measured and judged. How are Asian American Christians coping with the actuality of racism? What is their response to it in light of their faith? Following are some voices and signs that speak to these questions.

"To Feel the Pain": The Reminder of Imposed Tragedy

A full awareness of racism ripens our wisdom and deepens our understanding of life as Asian Americans. The racial philosophy that we must seek is a hard-eyed view of racism as it is and our subordinate role in it. "We must realize with our immigrant parents and grandparents that the struggle for freedom is, at bottom, a manifestation of our humanity that survives and grows stronger through resistance to oppression even if that oppression is never overcome," says Stephen Kim of the Center for Asian American Ministries at Claremont School of Theology in California. This hard-eyed view of racism tells us that societal stability is built on a belief in and a determination to maintain the dominance of those who are in positions of political, economic, and cultural power.

Racism serves as the manifestation of this deeply entrenched determination. Even a total reform of our economy or political system would not erase, and might even intensify, the need of the dominant group to measure its self-worth by keeping others in a subordinate status. "This nation is perceived as a nation of white, western European immigrants and their descendants. It is not sufficient, it is perceived, to be a child of God. It is necessary to be a white child of God. And that white child of God is somehow deemed, as a birthright, to fulfill a role of dominance. Therefore, anyone else—including Asian Americans—are perceived to be deemed an eternally tenuous place in this society."[15] This society is ordered, whether intentionally or not, in such a way that people of color are rendered powerless and barred from basic human rights, available goods, and equitable roles in shaping society. Such a reading of reality is neither a prescription for despair nor a counsel of surrender. Here, at least, is an honest and realistic perspective from which to gauge the present and future worth of our race-related activities. Freed of the stifling rigidity of "we shall overcome" thinking, we may be less ready to continue blindly our faith in traditional, integration-oriented remedies as the ideal, especially considering the evidence accrued over the years, that such policies seem to work only when it is in the interest of the dominant group for them to work.

Some Asian American Christians acknowledge (at least to ourselves) that our actions are unlikely to lead to transcendent change and, despite our best efforts, may be of more help to the system we despise than to the victims of that system. Such a realization can lead to positions that are less likely to worsen conditions of Asian Americans and other marginalized groups. Such a realization is also more likely to remind the powers-that-be that we are persons who are not on the side of oppression and are determined to stand in the way of the existing racist pattern. "To a great extent, the Asian movement for ethnic identity and consciousness has brought new awareness of responsibility for Asian [American] churches to become the advocates of their people and of others who are victims of racism and oppression. Whether the Asian [American] churches can meet this challenge in the future remains to be seen," observes Presbyterian pastor Nicholas Iyoya.[16] To be sure, it is not an approach without risks. But Asian Americans must face such a risk if we seek alternative possibilities to the racist reality of life in the United States.

The challenge is compounded, however, by the fact that Asian American Christians tend to be reticent in actively confronting racism. They "will largely ignore it and let it pass, or accept the status quo. They need to become aware of their need for corporate action and involvement to gain their ends," noted a Chicago area pastor.[17] The reason for it is the reality that Asian Americans have been by and large already acculturated into the Anglo-European culture. Here lies one of the ultimate claims of racism upon Asian Americans. The social system of North America allows Asian Americans, perhaps more than any other people of color, to access opportunities and to be assimilated into European American dominant culture. As a consequence, Asian Americans are perceived as a growing privileged class of people who can, and too often do, adapt to the European American way of life—grasping and striving for what Asian Americans think makes the dominant cultural group economically and socially successful. "But that makes Whites feel economically threatened and unwilling to share the wealth and power that Asians seem to be encroaching upon, and it makes other people of color hate them because they are so unnervingly 'White,' prejudiced and lacking in solidarity with other people of color," observes Maureen Lai-Ping Mark of Chicago.[18]

Moreover, Asian American professionals, having grown up in a system in which class identification is perceived as more important than race, are often astonished at the individual acts of racism directed against them. They expect their professional status to protect them. Even our churches have adopted the myth of power based on class identification. Asian American Christians' strife against racism in many ways has benefited an already upwardly mobile but legally constrained class of Asian Americans, without providing for the proper care and supportive services needed to enable the truly invisible underclass to have meaningful participation in American society. Perhaps the severest critique we can direct upon Asian American churches is that to a certain extent they have co-opted into the very racist structure of society and thus have come to neglect the most alienated people in society, the poor and underclass, even among our own Asian Americans.

Asian American churches have historically offered a wholistic vision for ministry. They have extended service to newly arrived immigrants and also have reached into our communities. But our entry into middle-class mainstream society has led us into radical structural differentiation and social class stratification reflective of the larger society. The price to be paid for middle-class advancement is found in our alienation from the poor within the Asian American community. In our effort to overcome racial subordination, Asian American churches have come to perpetuate the very ills of the society we critique. An Asian American minister who has long been a pioneer in the area of the church's social witness has pointed out that "the acculturation or assimilation and upward social and economic mobility of Asian Americans often results in the inability of many Asians to identify themselves with the forces combating racism and oppression."[19] An analogy that represents contemporary social arrangements between Asian American churches and the society as a whole is the Babylonian Exile, argue some Asian American Christians. In the Exile there was both a struggle with the Babylonian oppressor and an acknowledgment of the complicity of the oppressed in their own oppression. "The primary concern of the church seems to be institutional survival. The church has not made any systematic approach to social witness, Asian American or non-Asian," says Pastor Nicholas Iyoya.[20]

But if racial subordination is to a certain extent inevitable and unavoidable in this society, if all the efforts and accomplishments will come to little significance, then what is the worth of challenging racism? As discouraging as this questions sounds, it seems that when Asian American Christians ask the question honestly and aloud, we are dealing directly with the unstated question that has bedeviled Asian Americans all along. Out in the open, we can forthrightly look at the dilemma of the "meaning" of life and come to realize that meaning indeed ensues from meaningful activity, that meaningfulness emerges out of engagement and commitment. Nicholas Iyoya observes that some Asian American churches have gone into areas where other organizations have not ventured, such as a cooperative community-action program with a Buddhist church to fight against a racist school system. In other instances, they have worked in close cooperation with other community organizations. "Much of the progress in this area as well as other areas of the church depends on the quality and commitment of ministerial leadership and the presence of concerned laity."[21] In spite of the tendency of some Asian American churches to accept the status quo, there are churches which endeavor to be reconciled with the Asian American underclass community.

Such is the case for Buena Vista United Methodist Church in Alameda, California. This Japanese American church has faced the problem of urban renewal and its implication for the church and the community. Recently the home belonging to one of the church members and one belonging to a member of a nearby Chinese American congregation were subject to rezoning negotiations by the city of Alameda for the sake of a business enterprise. The church, under the leadership of pastor Michael Yoshii, responded to this challenge by developing a community organization, coalescing with other churches and organizations in the vicinity to confront the redevelopment agency and the city government. It was Pastor Yoshii's reading that racism against Asian Americans was an underlying factor in this rezoning concern. Even though the outcome is still undecided, the issue has become public, and an awareness of the concerns has emerged in the local community.

Presbyterian Church in Chinatown, San Francisco, has over the years developed aggressive programs that include a senior center, application for two hundred units of housing for moderate income families and senior citizens, affirmative action regarding employment, several youth programs, leadership training, and summer day camps, and provides leadership for other churches in the city. The church has been involved extensively in mental health, immigration, housing, tutorial programs, community organization, Asian American studies, youth, and employment opportunity. Ira Lee of Presbyterian Church reports of a Chinese congregation in the Bay Area that was instrumental in developing the Asian Community Council to cope with the issues arising among immigrants. The Mission Study Review Committee of the church stated that, "[l]ike other minorities, Asians are likewise involved in an identity quest. Unfortunately they are often times 'trapped' between the more publicized ethnic groups (between Anglos, Mexicans, and Blacks) and thus become 'invisible' and so ignored by the helping agencies, be they civic or ecclesiastical. Yet their needs are both real and intense."[22]

Amadeo Zarza, Presbyterian pastor in the heart of an agricultural region in California, led his church to an illustrious record of service to its people, many of whom are farm workers and small-shop owners. The church has provided a day care center for children of low-income families. The center serves Filipino mothers in the city, economically depressed families of other ethnic groups, and poor Anglo Americans. The church has made an effort to establish a credit union for Asian Americans in the county. Zarza states that 80 percent of the five thousand Filipinos in the county have no access to a credit union. The youths of this church have conducted a house-to-house survey in the city to collect data on housing, employment, education, and welfare needs. When asked about the adequacy of the church's response to the social needs of the time, Zarza replied, "The people respond to the degree that they themselves or their groups have been affected by the ills of society. The church should take these ills seriously and come up with practical solutions." In reference to the associations in this community, the pastor states that there are only 3,400 of his people in that city, and yet there are thirty-five associations, fraternities, and clubs in existence. "What these myriads of organizations reveal is the tendency of our people, and perhaps also among other ethnic groups, to divide and spread themselves thin, thus making themselves weak and directionless. Hopefully their participation in the denominational Asian Caucus will serve as a training ground for them to learn the lessons of unity, organization, and empowerment."[23]

These Asian American churches have come to recognize how difficult it is to have a positive effect on this country's continuing racial struggles. Those difficulties do not deter them, however, but give them reason to assess their realistic posture toward racism. Church leaders have come to realize that racial subordination will not end any time soon in this society. They have come to acknowledge through their own painful struggles that a yearning for racial equality is fantasy. Short of the extreme of a radical societal change, history and their personal experiences tell them that any forward step is likely either to drive Asian Americans backward eventually or to reinforce the myth that their efforts will be ultimately successful. Brian Ogawa, a Presbyterian, reminds Asian American Christians to "realize that [we] are indeed marginal people, who must be critical of social situations that [our] vision of wholeness and integrity obscure."[24]

What has emerged out of such a confrontation with the reality of racism through a Christian perspective is the recognition of both the futility of action and the dream of real, permanent racial equality and at the same time the firm conviction that action must be taken. Nevertheless, Asian American Christians go on confronting the ills of racism. It is a curious contradiction that speaks powerfully about the faith conviction of Asian American Christians. It is a faith assessment that calls for learning how to survive the unbearable landscape and climate of truth. Challenged by the reality of racial conditions, Asian American Christians and churches are attempting to extract solutions from our survival even as we suffer what is often insurmountable despair.

Together with other Christians of color, Asian Americans addressed the reality of racism in the United States at the International Consultation on Racism and Racial Justice in 1988. The statement that emerged from the conference speaks of a racism that permeated even into the structure of churches:

> We are deeply pained. The response of the Churches has been a deafening silence. Ecumenical bodies have failed to share power and instead model hierarchical, racially exclusive structures rather than structures that point toward the beloved community. There was a day when Church leaders were identified by their stand on issues of racial justice—where are they now! There was a day when ecumenical bodies were at the forefront of the struggle for racial justice—where are they now! There was a day when our national leaders felt compelled to signal to the world that this nation intended to make real our vision of equality and justice—where are they now![25]

The Christians gathered in Los Angeles covenanted together and issued an open letter to all churches. "[W]e demand that the Churches from their hierarchy to the local congregations listen to the stories of racial injustice from the plurality of people in their pews and in the world, and to feel their pain."[26] It was a resolution to continue the fight against racism even in their acknowledgment of its insidious and tenacious nature.

"Feel their pain!" is not only Asian American Christians' call to all the churches. It also speaks of the courage and strength of Christians of color to confront racism head-on. It is intended to infuse the reality of tragedy into the very reading of the life of those who wear a racial uniform. To "feel the pain" is to strive toward the basic form of humanity, the "sacred bond," with little to help save imagination, will, and firm resolution and courage. Beating the odds while firmly believing in the equality of all people, knowing as only they could that all those odds were stacked against them, they still go on.

Such a posture is alien to the prevailing culture of what has been referred to as the "Officially Optimistic Society" of North America.[27] In the positive outlook of life prevailing in this society, the notion of "pain" sounds both masochistic and non-utilitarian. Nevertheless, it is true to the reading of reality given through the life experiences of Asian American Christians. The ethos of mastery, which is the foundation of the positive outlook of life, is foreign to those who are on the fringes of society. Instead, the experience of negation, particularly in the form of racism, predominates the basic ethos of Asian Americans. The gospel of Christ is not to be seen as a word that meets, answers, conquers, and so annuls the negative. Rather, it is a vantage point from which to engage the negative; to engage it, not to overcome it. The community of faith is the place in which we deal with our questions of the negative, not a place in which we will find an answer. Not the overcoming of the negative, but the possibility of engaging it, of encountering it at the level of conscious reflection, of facing it in all its enormity, is the primary endeavor of the faith.

Asian American Christians are convinced that there is something real in this society for us. It is not, though, the "romantic love" of integration—though like romance, we may seek and sometimes experience it. It is surely not the long-sought goal of equality under law—though we must maintain the struggle against racism else the erosion of rights becomes even worse than it now is. The conviction of Asian American Christians is a hard-eyed view of racism as it is and our subordinate role in it. We realize with our immigrant parents and grandparents that the struggle for freedom is, at bottom, a manifestation of our humanity that survives and grows stronger through resistance to oppression, even if that oppression is never overcome.

David Hirano, chief executive of the United Church Board for World Ministries, describes Asian American experiences of racism in terms of the feeling of shame: "Every person who is of racial and ethnic minority in the United States knows what shame is. . . . Those who have experienced defeat in any sense have experienced shame. Shame is disgraced. Shame is feeling 'the eyes of the world' upon them. Shame is feeling unworthy. Shame is experienced when the dominant culture interprets silence as ignorance or stupidity. Shame is trying to hide one's ethnicity. Sometimes shame exhibits itself in working extra hard to be a United States citizen while not being treated as one."[28] The faith community is the setting in which the shameful experience of racism is endured. "It is to live in community without bringing shame upon it," says Hirano.[29] It is also to live in community with honesty and the courage to confront shame. Shame, in other words, is a painful expression of truth about life in this society. Truth comes necessarily from those who are excluded and disfranchised from mainstream society in their expressions of painful shame. The faith community for Asian American Christians offers in this officially optimistic society a new paradigm for dealing with the experience of negation in the form of shame. Through our experiences of racism we have come to understand, perhaps more intuitively than cognitively, that the gospel never indulges in the sort of instant overcoming of evil that characterizes so much of Christian thought. On the contrary, the way to overcome evil involves a more intensive encounter with it.

The explicit weakness of kerygmatic triumphalism is that it makes it very difficult, if not quite impossible, to take seriously the evil that is present in life. The critical theological challenge of Asian American churches is to extricate the biblical confession of the divine triumph *pro nobis* from the triumphalistic worldview of European American bourgeois society. The test of theological authenticity is whether we can present Jesus as the one who knows the experience of negation, marginalization, and the anguish of hopelessness. Would we dare to confess to this Jesus our deepest anxieties, our most ultimate questions? Would he, the God-Human of this faith-thinking, be able to weep over the anguish of Korean American and African American shop owners in South Central Los Angeles, as he wept over Lazarus? The test of authenticity in theology is: Is this "Christ and him crucified"? A victory that does not annul his defeat, to leave the cross "empty," a void, a meaningless symbol. If there is a God, God would have to be "with us" in the agony and failure of our humanity, in our experience of racism and its seeming hopelessness. If that were so we would not have to look for meaning beyond our suffering and shame, but in them: in the midst of negation of life, a way; in the midst of despair, hope. A primary theological task for Asian American Christians is to provide a frame of reference for our experience of negation. The only hope that would be pertinent to our condition and responsible within the context of North American society would be one that is born out of an honest encounter with the despair implicit in and emanating from our own way of life.

The Pathos of Justice: A Critique of the Consensus

There is a woundedness in speaking of truth. To strive for justice in the face of racism essentially means to critique the prevailing consensus and to search for an alternative vision of human relatedness based on experiences of pain and suffering. The perceptions and practices of a people with power has become a settled formula to define and legitimate a closed, encapsulated system. Racial justice advocated by Asian American Christians is meant to move against the old tradition and prevailing conventions. Such a disruption comes from nonlegitimated sources because the closed circle between the existing convention and its proponents is broken and shattered only by a new voice which has no such vested interest. The challenge for racial justice is therefore likely to be a cry from the powerless and disinherited. It is likely to come from those who feel the pain of exclusion. Racial justice breaks through out of pain, exasperation, rage, incredulity, and irrationality. The cry for justice breaks the rationality and shatters the universe of discourse that legitimates the present order. "Pacific and Asian-Americans are also a people with 'pathos'— with stories of deep pain and suffering. A primary source of this pathos is to be found in the racism encountered in America," points out Presbyterian Wesley Woo.[30] Amidst the history of violence, massacre, internment, and discriminatory legislation with regards to immigration, taxation, land ownership, and miscegenation, Asian American Christians cry out for justice. "The Christian Church must be held culpable in all this too."[31]

United Methodist Bishop Roy Sano critiques the "central and most telling symbol for U.S. Protestantism," that of levitating crosses in the sanctuaries of churches. The original intent of the suspended cross was to keep the person of Christ from becoming immersed in the evil and sin of this world. But this symbol highlighted his divinity and neglected his humanity. "When it comes to the work of Christ in U.S. Protestantism, we emphasize the triumph of the resurrection succeeding the tragedy of the cross. Thus the levitating cross depicts the triumph but not the continuing involvement of Christ in our struggles, or of suffering and resurrection occurring simultaneously. A theology of struggle from an Asian American perspective suggests we challenge these heretical icons or call for a crucifix if we must suspend the cross in the sanctuary."[32] In making this criticism of the implicit triumphalism of so much of the Protestant church's preaching and practice, Asian American Christians do not mean

to deny the power of the gospel to transform the human condition. But there is a certain modesty in our reading of the
Gospel that has been almost lost in Christendom: the Gospel
never indulges in the sort of instant overcoming of evil which
characterizes so much of traditional Christian thought. There is
always a "not yet" in the biblical witness. Moreover, there is a
deep awareness that the final overcoming of evil involves us in a
yet more intensive encounter with it that does not exclude feeling pain.

Our cry for justice is directed toward reestablishing human
relatedness and community in situations of suffering. "Feelings of
discomfort or uneasiness in the present society and feelings of not
belonging can be channeled towards working for God's purposes,
instead of towards searching for personal security and acceptance
into society. . . . [T]his sojourner lifestyle has direction. We can
be led by the possibilities of the fullness of the realm of God. It
can captivate us so much that it keeps us ever moving forward.
'The Kingdom of Heaven is like a merchant in search of fine
pearls, who, on finding one pearl of great value, went and sold all
that he had and bought it' (Matt. 13:45)."[33]

As racism disrupts the basic form of human relatedness and
community, justice moves us toward the reestablishment of community. "[I]t is important to remember that it is God who calls,
sustains, and judges us in our lives as sojourners. To lose sight of
this is to lose any sense of direction and to become aimless
wanderers or to retreat to search for personal comfort and security alone," says a group of Asian American Presbyterians.[34] This
is reminiscent of the words of Karl Barth, who insisted that the
entire "happening" of the basic form of humanity "stands under
the sign that it happens . . . gladly [gerne]."[35] The opposite of
"gladly" is not simply "unwillingly" but "neutrally" and thus cyni-
cally, argues theologian Benjamin Reist.[36] Cynicism is the real
enemy of the basic form of human relatedness. It is crucially
important to remember that "it is God who calls, sustains, and
judges us" in our move toward the reestablishment of community
and thus the basic form of humanity. In the articulation of life in
the gospel then, the visible integrity of the basic form of human-

ity is recognized. Striving for justice is inseparable with one's faith affirmation.

"A theology of struggle" is an expression of such a posture among Asian American Christians. "A theology of struggle is an integral part of our participation in God's creative and saving drama. The sojourn involves setbacks and suffering. The sojourn could hallow the life of a person who has known the sacrilege of a life violated, a desecration of people exploited, ours and others as well, including white Americans."[37] Striving for racial justice is an affirmation of the basic form of humanity. What is distinct about Asian American Christians' view is that this form of humanity is conditioned by cultural formation, which seems to stress the notion of harmony and reciprocity among all people and all creation. There appears to be a pervasive influence of the neo-Confucian value formation among many Asian Americans, particularly those in earlier generations of Chinese Americans, Japanese Americans, and Korean Americans. Christian communities do not escape its impact. Asian American Christians tend intuitively to view an alternative way of human relatedness that is less bipolar in nature and directed more toward a whole of all beings. "The individual is not as important as the group itself. . . . 'Harmony' is a virtue; confrontation makes unnecessary waves," characterizes Maureen Lai-Ping Mark.[38]

Triumph in Defiance: A Theology of Struggle

The simple proclamation of the gospel of reconciliation and harmony is not enough to affect the racist society. The focus of need is on the basic form of humanity that is distorted and corrupted. Being related one with another without exclusion, domination, and alienation can never happen "gladly" when the reality of racism blocks the fulfillment of the I-thou relationship. The distortion and ruin of racism have exhibited disturbing outcomes in South Central Los Angeles, New York City, and numerous other cities of this nation in recent months and years. "The three-day madness in Los Angeles had nothing to do with us Korean Americans," says Eui-Young Yu. "It was a violent explosion of anger accumulated over centuries of frustration, helplessness, and alienation of the people of color in this country."[39] The inescapable truth is that our national symbols are tainted by the racism associated with the nation's founding and development. Until the very fabric of the society is challenged, injustice will perpetuate the relationships among groups that make up the society and violence will raise its ugly head at every available opportunity. "The very stones will cry out," inevitably, in a racist society, and have.

The acculturation and upward social and economic mobility of Asian Americans, however, tend to result in the inability of many to identify with the forces combating racism. Furthermore, the primary concern of Asian American churches tends to be institutional survival. It is difficult for them to make any concerted effort at approaching issues of racial justice. Coupled with the tenacity of racist forces that are woven into the very fabric of this society, the challenge facing Asian American churches is enormous.

But the stones do cry out. The challenges to confront racism are being articulated in light of the Asian American Christian community's experience of faith. Racial justice for Christians has an intrinsically religious character which is manifested in community. "Even if we were part of a system which benefited us personally, as Moses, Esther, and Daniel discovered, a society which hosted us favorably could exploit and oppress our own people. . . . A sense of 'being had' despite our acceptance and gains explains some of the animus behind the Asian American participation in the racial struggles. What we discovered in the movement led some of us to dig deeper into the roots of our faith," says Bishop Sano.[40] This is reminiscent of Martin Luther King, Jr. Dr. King insisted that any valid attempt to understand the centrality of Jesus for all Christian thought must entail an explicit relating of "the name [Jesus] to the concrete affairs of men."[41] Filipino Methodist pastor Ruth Cortez reflects on an emerging theology of struggle among Filipino and Filipino Americans:

> [T]he theology that is emerging and is being articulated out of
> the matrix of the suffering and struggles of the people, is being
> given shape, form, embodiment, language, symbolism and
> imagery by those who have the wounds in their hands and
> feet, the scars in their sides and heads, those who have learned
> to wipe away their tears and to keep their voices from weep-
> ing, and address themselves to the laborious and dangerous
> tasks of organizing, educating, and consciousness-raising, of
> mobilizing a greater number of our people to participate in the
> long and protracted march to liberation and wholeness.[42]

The norm of theological talk here is inseparably linked with the
very existence of Asian Americans and our life struggles. This is
particularly true in our facing the reality of racism. The link
between theology and racism needs to be handled with great
care, for it touches on the dynamics of a process now only in its
formative phases, and all that is currently discernible is the com-
mencement of tasks that will continue for a long time. Is it
possible to go further than polemics?

To pose the question in this fashion is to encounter its
complexity. Likely to be characteristic of efforts along this line of
inquiry is an ambivalence of theological enterprise, necessitated
by the fact that the power of racism remains so overwhelming.
This power is no less observable within the realm of the theological establishment than it is elsewhere in the world of the dominant culture. Accordingly, any constructive theological effort
utilizing hitherto ignored or suppressed sources of creativity and
discernment will continue to be combined with the maintenance
of polemical pressure. The theological expression and articulation of Asian American Christians risks the danger of being
ignored and contained by those who resist the change we demand. An alternative to the "unconventional" and sometimes
offensive theological expression of Asian American Christians in
the face of racism is containment and trivialization.

Moreover, the ever-present pain of racism demands no less
than theology's acknowledgment of it:

When I was young kids used to ask me what are you?
I'd tell them what my mom told me, I'm an American
chin chin chinaman, you're a Jap!
flashing hot inside I'd go home my mom would say,
don't worry, he who walks alone walks faster
people kept asking me what are you? and I would always
answer I'm an American
they'd say, no, what nationality?
I'm an American, that's where I was born flashing hot inside
and when I'd tell them what they wanted to know Japanese
. . . Oh, I have been to Japan I'd get it over with
so they could catalogue and file me, pigeon-hole me
so they'd know just
how to think of me priding themselves they could guess the
difference between Japanese and Chinese
they had me wishing I was what I'd been seeing on movies and
on T.V., on billboards and in magazines
and I tried while they were making laws in California
against us owning land
we were trying to be American
and laws against us intermarrying with white people we were
trying to be American when they put us in concentration
camps we were trying to be American our people volunteered
to fight against their own country trying to be American
when they dropped the atom bomb on Hiroshima and Nagasaki we
were still trying.
finally we made it most of our parents fiercely dedicated to
give us a good education, to give us everything they never
had we made it now they use us as an example to the blacks
and browns how we made it, how we overcame now I answer, I'm
an Asian and they say, why do you want to separate

yourselves now I say I'm Japanese and they say
don't you know this is the greatest country in the world
now I say, in America I'm part of the third world people
and they say, if you don't like it here why don't you go
back to where you came from![43]

This is the reality theology cannot ignore in order to claim its own validity and legitimacy. The most crucial ingredient of Asian American Christians' faith reflection is our historicity, and particularly the pathos associated with it. Reflecting on his Japanese heritage with its propensity toward the impact of suffering, Bishop Sano says: "In this theology of struggle, the Japanese focus on suffering and death is being fitted into the shape of the Christian story of death and resurrection of Jesus. In turn this part of the story portends the climactic reign of life over death, thus the perspective is Asian and 'American.'"[44]

The struggle against racism is, at bottom, a manifestation of our humanity that survives and grows stronger through resistance to oppression, even if that oppression is never overcome. The basic posture is defiance pursued with full knowledge of the power of racism and its continuing presence regardless of our effort to fight against it. Defiance against oppression and racism is in itself triumph. The theology of struggle articulates this basic posture of Asian American Christians. "Power and greed will ravage beauty and give us loneliness. But all this will come to pass. So live the New Year flooding the city with noises, like the tragic noises of revolution, that reach me like a heartstroke. And all will move forward on the indiscriminate course of history that never stops to rectify our tragic misgivings and shame."[45]

Toward Reconciliation and Transformation: Reestablishment of Community

Defiance, however, is not sufficient. Defiance is not an expression of the "basic form of humanity." The needed task is to create alternatives to the existing power perception of humanity, to transform the image, and ask ourselves questions about ways of relating one group with another that move us away from dualistic and bipolar thinking about humanity. In order to live as human beings in this society, what is needed is a reexamination of the existing form of humanity and the envisioning of a new form. "[R]acism permeates all the institutions of society, to the point that often it is not seen for what it is," points out Wesley Woo.[46]

The primary issue of racism in the United States is inequality based on domination and the resultant estrangement of, for the most part, the poor and underclass. Racial/ethnic or cultural prejudice by the dominant group against Asian Americans and other peoples of color is only secondary. "The ultimate ethnic myth, perhaps, is the belief that the cultural symbols of the past can provide more than a comfortable illusion to shield us from present-day discontents," reminds Stephen Steinberg in the book *Ethnic Myth*.[47] The central issues of racism have less to do with the distinctness of Asian American culture or ethnicity than with economic policy, social rule, and class relations that undermine our well-being. The challenge is to speak that which has not been spoken and to find a new vision of relationship and social order among those who exist in the world of power asymmetry.

Racism is indeed a structural subsystem of domination. It interacts with other subsystems to produce broad patterns of oppression and exploitation. The aim of Asian Americans' striving for racial justice is, then, to join in an effort to create the basis for healing the national wounds, even if to do so we must "hope against hope." James Baldwin, writing in *The Fire Next Time*, crystallized the matter: "In order to survive as a human, moving, moral weight in the world, America and all the Western nations will be forced to reexamine themselves and release themselves from many things that are now taken to be sacred, and to discard nearly all the assumptions that have been used to justify their lives and their anguish and their crimes so long."[48]

This is to say that a primary issue at stake in the fight against racism is the reactionary restructuring of our understanding of mutual responsibilities within a society. Individual autonomy and differentiation comprise our predominant societal values and are in direct opposition to any egalitarian posture of human relatedness. An absolute individual liberties posture undercuts commitments to the shared good and ignores the fact that this country has always felt it important and necessary to give special attention to particular groups such as veterans. The possibility of mutual interdependence of all people is undermined by a tremendous resistance to any attempt toward racial justice, preferential treatment, or affirmative action. Opposition toward racial equality is at bottom a linguistic smokescreen for an agenda aimed at maintaining the status quo and refusing to take on the arduous and admittedly complex and delicate task of rooting out systematic and institutional injustice—injustice that to the victims of discrimination is still all too apparent.

Where do Asian American churches begin their challenge to racism? It begins with a search for mutual partnerships in ministry with congregations that are already engaged in significant ministry in impoverished communities. Joint ministry projects, which model the commitment of the congregations to each other, would flow out of the relationships developed by the congregations. The yoke cannot be forged by the ministry projects themselves, however well intentioned they are, for the churches would then lapse into that false anthropology that defines our humanity by accomplishments rather than by human relatedness. It is in worshiping, playing, praying, and "fellowshiping" together with those who are less privileged that relationships are developed, whereby in feeling one another's pain people minister to one another. The key in all of this is the primacy of relationships, not programs. If churches enter into relationships with the underclass in whatever ways they can, ministry will flow as a natural response to the needs of others, rather than as some charitable but unloving act. The plight of those who are on the fringe of society impoverishes not only them but also those who are protected from such a plight.

Unfortunately, U.S. society has yet to comprehend fully the importance of racial, ethnic, underrepresented, and underprivileged peoples to the future well-being of all Americans. Perhaps, just perhaps, the church could become a necessary channel to break the cycle of racial despair and the ever-widening fragmentation of human groupings in this society based on class and race. The pathos of Asian American experiences of racism may well become a motivating force to keep Asian American Christians from perpetuating the very pain they experience—that is, pain in the form of ignoring those who are underprivileged and disfranchised in today's society. This is a real challenge for the ministry and mission of Asian American churches.

Christ Church of Chicago, United Church of Christ, was born out of the suffering of Japanese American Christians. The church was founded largely by those who were relocated following the camp experiences soon after the end of World War II. The pathos of life experienced in internment contributed deeply to the forming of its community culture and ethos. The church is particularly noted for its extensive involvements in community affairs in Chicago: the ecumenical Night Ministry program, two homeless shelters, the annual Hunger Walk, the retirement and nursing homes for Japanese American elderly, wellness and parish nurse programs, and the Community Renewal Society. The "Tri-C" is also a very vital congregation with informal and highly energetic worship services every Sunday. The lay leadership is largely made up of capable nisei people. Sansei members have also begun to assume leadership both in the nurturing of the congregation and in their outreach programs. The foundation for this active parish and the mission involvements of its members derives largely from their internment experiences and their highly developed sense of empathy and compassion for those who are in need, both within their own community and in the wider community of the city of Chicago. The values that govern the congregation's culture are deeply formed by its members' experiences of pathos and willingness to reach out to those who live on the fringe of the society.

The ordering of life for those who experience the deep and profound pain of racism takes on an unconventional dimension when compared to those who occupy the dominant power position in the society. H. Richard Niebuhr reminded us of this as early as 1929 in his *Social Sources of Denominationalism:* "The religion of the untutored and economically disfranchised classes has distinct ethical and psychological characteristics, corresponding to the needs of these groups. . . . The salvation which it seeks and sets forth is the salvation of the socially disinherited."[49] The faith of Asian American Christians could also motivate us to see life not only descriptively, thereby recognizing pain, but also critically, calling into account the religious, cultural, and economic structures that cause the pain and suffering of racism. We have seen the fluid and complex nature of the Asian American search for an identity. What this experience of Asian Americans indicates is the fundamental ambiguity and at the same time the dynamic ordering of life. Any claim for centrality at the cost of the well-being of others, or assertion of power that denies the freedom of those with whom life is to be shared is suspect. The ordering of life in this fashion, moreover, is likely to be expressed in terms of a shift in value orientation. It is, in fact, the experience and acceptance of an ambiguous and dynamic state of life that allows the transformation of values and worldview.

The pain of being a "minor key" leads to the promise of the fair and just relatedness of all humanity based on an honest acknowledgment of disparity among people. Such a relatedness is an "impossible possibility" that Asian Americans experience when we come to an honest acknowledgment and confession of the basic disparate state of human life. But,

> "*No man is an island, entire of itself; every one is a piece of the Continent, a part of the main. . . ." Part of what binds us closest together as human beings and makes it true that no one is an island is the knowledge that in another way every one is an island, alone. Because to know this is to know that not only deep in you is there a self that longs above all to be known and accepted, but there is also such a self in me, in everyone else the world over. So when I meet strangers, when even our friends and loved ones look like strangers, it is good to remember that we need each other greatly you and I, more*

than much of the time we dare to imagine, more than most of
the time we dare to admit.[50]

As these words of both John Donne and Frederick
Buechner reveal, a prerequisite to human reconciliation and fair
and just relationships is the courage to meet strangers on common ground. The foundation of social life is not the forging of a
common historical identity but the capacity of people located in
an asymmetrical power structure to share a common territory,
common resources, and common problems—without becoming
similar in outlook and without subjugating one to another. The
emergence of such a society requires the passage of "time which
resolves problems through supplanting them by new problems,
and through the . . . generation of new traditions which only the
passage of time can nurture."[51] Striving for such a vision of
society requires a courage that is fundamentally confessional in
character and is likely to emerge out of an experience of the deep
pain of diversity, out of one's experience of being an "island." It is
from an experience of the profound pain of disparity and estrangement that the yearning for the reconciled, basic form of
humanity derives. William Greenbaum is not far from the truth
when he says that "the past exclusion of minority and Third
World people from the western mainstream may turn out to be
humanity's greatest hope."[52] It is, however, only those who have
undergone the pain of pluralism and the alienation of asymmetrical relationships who can utter such words with legitimacy and
authenticity. Asian American Christians' quest for the affirmation of our beings begins with a desire for an ethnic self-
definition.

But our probing into the depths quickly brings us to the
realization that our quest is also shared by other ethnic, social, and ancestral peoples of underrepresentation. We discover
that Asian Americans share matters with African Americans,
Hispanic Americans, American Indians, Pacific Islanders, and
others: All of us are anxious about the prospects for our lives. We
struggle in common with inadequacy, deviancy, and marginality;
we experience small victories; we enjoy the pleasure of being in

harmony with others and being at peace with ourselves. We have to come to terms with our loneliness, even while living in familiar places. We suffer. One of the profound discoveries is that there is indeed a stranger within ourselves. Somehow this experience of commonality among all people brings some Asian American Christians to utter the words which are truly the glue that holds all people together in the midst of estrangement and alienation. Here exists the redemptive power of the suffering and pain of Asian American Christians. In the words of Paul Nagano, a Japanese American Baptist pastor: "We have been placed in internment camp. Our stories are full of suffering and pain. And yet, I am deeply convinced that we have to go beyond rage, resentment, and fear of those who placed us into such predicament. We all must live together."[53] When we live out of such a confession, we find the glue that holds us together.

The experience of "rage, resentment, and fear" is an opportunity that could lead to new cognition, new epistemologies, and new ways of knowing and naming reality. The movement from pain and suffering caused by racism to a new vision of humanity requires painful lessons in memory and accountability. It requires a yearning, passion, and a determination to know what has occurred, and at the same time, a will to move beyond bondage to past experience into a vision of a new and alternative ordering of human relationships. When the people who are historically recipients of imposed suffering find their voices and begin to speak for themselves it brings about new interpretations of traditional symbols and texts, new analyses of social structures, critiques of the institutional structure of the society, and solidarity with others. Asian American Christians who have undergone the historically imposed suffering of racism are speaking out. "We can understand the past not as authoritative judgment, but as a complex, unromanticized memory of who we are and where we have been. It is not a tyranny, but a resource for understanding. People are not simply victims to be pitied or helped, but agents of their own lives, survivors who are neither innocent nor good, but who, within the limits of power given them, make conscious willed choices for good and ill," says Asian American theologian Rita

Nakashima Brock.[54] These are prophetic voices in the ongoing struggle to create and enflesh Christian faith, which strengthens the bonds of community. Their voices are subversive to the existing social order because they challenge the status quo and yearn for a new and more harmonious social order based on transformed human relationships. Their voices are indeed visionary voices.

Visionary voices are a powerful force in the building of resistance to racism and of hope-filled communities. However, voices that speak of a vision of the future are scarce because they require the tenacity to move through oppression and victimization, sacrifice and resentment, and grief and sorrow and still maintain the resolve to tell the story. This level of resistance is scarce because of the tendency of the victim of racism to internalize oppression and accept the definition of self put forward by the dominant social and cultural power. Human dignity can and has been effectively neutralized or destoryed in individuals and groups. People who are victims of racism need to constantly struggle against defeatism and a negative self-image. Those who are able to live with dignity are often the ones who muster the courage to tell the story while not being shouted down in the process.

Recipients of injustice often express the feeling that they have survived in order that the story can be told and remembered. "I was God's wonder boy: but if I did not defile the greed of mad men, if I did not save beauty from the naked blasphemies of money, you must know that I cried when the Jews were driven from their country, when the Negroes were burned in their homes. You must know that with these feeble hands I crept to the window unashamed to die in a world gone mad with power," says Filipino American poet Carlos Bulosan.[55] History is rooted in the stories and memories that are told and remembered. History is not "what happened" but "what shall be remembered." When Asian Americans tell the stories of our experiences of racism we are not just seeking personal healing but are also creating resurrection memory in human history. In that sense, we are literally the carriers of visionary memories. Our stories are a collective source of resistance and struggle. Our stories embody resurrection memory: the hope for transformation and new life.

It is the life, death, and resurrection of Jesus that grounds Christian memory. "Do this as oft as ye drink it, in remembrance of me" is the call to all of the Christian community that celebrates the bread and cup. It represents the centrality of remembrance to the life of the Christian community. The eucharist becomes visionary memory when it is understood as a transformative symbol, remembering the one who embodied struggle and resistance to oppressive social, cultural, and political structures. The eucharist does not point toward visionary memory when it is understood to represent a Jesus who willingly suffered and sacrificed himself through mere obedience.

Sim Togasaki was one who carried such a visionary memory. He and his family were relocated from their Berkeley home in California to an internment camp at the outbreak of World War II. Following their internment and eventual relocation to Chicago, which was assisted by the Church of the Brethren, they were returned to the Bay Area in the spring of 1946. On Maundy Thursday of that year, they went to Oakland Church of the Brethren for the celebration of Love Feast. There Sim sat next to a European American Brethren missionary who was on his way home from China where he and his family were interned by Japanese occupation troops. It was Sim who washed the feet of this missionary at the Love Feast, based on the story in the thirteenth chapter of the Gospel of John. When the two men stood face-to-face following the feet-washing and embraced each other with a holy kiss, Sim recalls, something happened to his bitter experience of the past. What defined human relationships for him was no longer estrangement based on resentment and fear and anger caused by the injustice done to Japanese Americans. Rather, it became the divine gift of grace which is the restoration of human relatedness, which defies even historical imposed suffering. This vision of an alternative order of human communal life is rooted in historical consciousness and biblical memory and enacted in the service of the Love Feast. Estrangement and alienation cannot be easily erased between Sim

Togasaki and the missionary. But they no longer function as the defining power of what it means to be human. The "basic form of humanity" came to have its power over both men in the service of the Love Feast. Historical consciousness is rooted in the particular stories of the biblical past. It is there that contemporary stories of struggle become an indispensable tool for biblical reappropriation. It is the historical stories of the silenced voices of injustice that let us know about the silenced voices of today and injustice and violence of racism present in this world. The proper starting point of a just world is therefore the juxtaposition of historical consciousness that hears the silenced voices and biblical remembrance that recaptures the meaning of Scripture as understood by the silenced. It is the concrete stories of those who suffer racism in the struggle for liberation that form the bases for transformative biblical interpretation. Rita Nakashima Brock's "hermeneutics of wisdom," while going beyond biblical history into the historical and cultural world of Asia, nevertheless speaks to the issue. Brock's hermeneutics of wisdom "interprets the past by refusing nothing that might help sustain life and pass it on, but which is also suspicious of mystification. The hermeneutics of wisdom helps create understanding and build community at the same time that it does not mystify authority."[56]

A gathering of Asian and Asian American women seminarians took place at Stony Point, New York, in 1991. There the women talked about "inheriting our mothers' gardens," the expression coined after the name of a book by Christian women. Reflecting on their experiences of racism and sexism, they said: "[W]e were not comfortable and were reluctant to inherit our mother's garden, because it was the garden of oppression, exploitation, domination, inferiority and disempowerment and so on. Nevertheless, we felt it was important to remember our mother's gardens in order to liberate and empower our present and future lives. We are looking forward to cultivating gardens full of varieties of vegetables, flowers, and plants."[57] History is not by itself redemptive but it has a capacity for being changed from within. Incarnational grace is the force that propels the power to overcome given dehumanizing historical conditions. "In the struggle of life, we discussed two different gardens and ended up redis-covering and liberating our mother's gardens which were hidden by patriarchal and other forces of oppression," the women said.[58] Grace is rooted in the embodied experience of the pain of racism and sexism turning into the experience of right relationship. Grace is located within people in history in places where creative transformation is occurring. Grace is experienced in healing acts of compassion and vision for an alternative future. It is lived experience that confirms the presence or absence of grace.

This grace is sustained by narrative. Grace is manifested in the stories, past and present, of resistance, struggle, healing, and transformation. Remembering the Exodus narrative can be a source for grace. Remembering the Gospel narratives can be a source for grace. However, incarnational grace does not stop with the remembering of biblical stories but integrates biblical narra-tive with ongoing historical experience. Grace becomes manifest in the collective narratives of life, the ongoing narratives which keep hope, struggle, and resistance alive in the lives of people. "Though arriving at the end of our first century and celebrating it, we still are seekers. . . . Our fathers crossed over the Pacific for a new life in this land; they were immigrants, away from their homes. They found what the life of sojourners was like, and yet, wherever they were, they were not away from the Lord's field. They met him, and built their churches."[59] If the story is not told, grace will wither and fade. The power of narrative, the story told, is the power which sustains embodied grace. Grace as the concrete historical and incarnational experience of Christians shatters imposed silence, restores the will to know, incorporates the rage of historical victims, and calls for new ways of knowing and naming reality. The struggle is always unfinished; there is always need for grace because there is always more that needs to be done. "We still are a pursuing church, or the pilgrim of God in the wilderness, or the dispersed like the first century Christians, or simply call it *search*—we are all on the way, together."[60]

≋ 4
Conclusion

*There is a silence that cannot speak. There is a silence that will
not speak. Beneath the grass the speaking dreams and beneath
the dreams is a sensate sea. The speech that frees comes forth
from that amniotic deep. To attend its voice, I can hear it say, is
to embrace its absence. But I fail the task. The word is
stone. . . . Unless the stone bursts with telling, unless the seed
flowers with speech, there is in my life no living word. The sound
I hear is only sound. White sound. Words, when they fall, are
pock marks on the earth. They are hailstones seeking an underground stream. If I could follow the stream down and down to
the hidden voice, would I come at last to the freeing word? I ask
the night sky but the silence is steadfast. There is no reply.[1]*

To attend to the voice of the silent one "is to embrace its absence." Joy Kogawa in her novel *Obasan* attempts to wrestle with
the question of an alternative and different way of being from
that which conventionally prevails in society. The novel treats
the interrelation between the subject of the "I" and the language
through which the subject is revealed. The theme of recovering a

lost mother is revealed through the thematics of the recuperative powers of language itself. In tracing "being," as constituted both in silence and in language, the main character of the novel is concerned with how a voice or its silence maintains or breaks down societal and cultural repressions that exist in North America. In the words of Johann Herder, language has a "living spirit" that is brought to bear upon society's considerations of the place a particular group of people has in nature.

Even in silence, however, the voice does not become muted. Silent or silenced ones still pose questions that do not go unheard. There is a powerful message in silence itself. In *Obasan*, the re-creation of the lost mother is the culmination of the narration of the daughter's story, which is also the story of the writer who has to overcome the silence of her ethnic community in order to create her text and her identity. The mother's silence is that of "amniotic deep," of "speaking dreams" from which comes "the speech that frees." Kogawa finds the resonance of such silence in the Gospel of John: "You shall know the truth and the truth shall make you free." Truth is conflated with "speaking dreams." The freeing speech comes from underground, from the subconscious, and is associated with the period of unity between child and mother.

Kogawa's question speaks to Asian Americans and our grappling with life in America today: What is the way of being that brings about a basic change in the patterns of human interrelationships that have historically enhanced the welfare of some and silenced of others? How do we break out of the patterns of human relationships that have resulted in oppression of certain groups of people and in alienation among those who make up this society? Kogawa's question speaks of the place of Asian Americans in this increasingly polarized and racially charged society of today.

In 1969, following a long summer of racial unrest in the nation's cities, the presidentially appointed Kerner Commission warned that the United States was "moving toward two societies, one black, one white—separate and unequal." In 1992, in an eerie reprise of that summer's events, violent disturbances in Los

Angeles, as well as in New York, Detroit, and other U.S. cities, made the commission's prediction seem almost quaint. It was clear from the images of African Americans, European Americans, Latinos, and Asian Americans confronting each other in the streets that America is not two societies, but multiple societies, each disparate from the others. A mere quarter of a century since the Kerner Commission Report, racial and ethnic alienation is perhaps one of the most denied realities in America. It was indeed a violent explosion of anger accumulated over a long period of frustration and alienation that the people of color have experienced. Our situations are increasingly becoming explosive.

In 1903, W. E. B. Du Bois predicted that the problem of the twentieth century would be the problem of the color line. As we reach the end of the century, the problem is "the problem of ethnic differences, as these conspire with complex differences in color, gender, and class," says Henry Louis Gates, Jr.[2] The question arising out of Kogawa's novel *Obasan* speaks to this situation: What is an alternative way of being and relating with one another amid highly charged interracial and interethnic tension and alienation? As cultural differences are brought to bear to justify the subordination of various groups of people by another, creating an increasingly alarming alienation among the diverse groups of people who make up U.S. society, Kogawa's question speaks directly to the heart of the matter that concerns us most.

The issue cannot be treated simply. Even those who are concerned with the interracial and interethnic alienation in this society often see it as one of many equally pressing societal problems rather than the issue that informs all other problems in America. "Instead of a nation composed of individuals making their own free choices, America increasingly sees itself as composed of groups more or less indelible in their ethnic character. The national ideal had once been *e pluribus unum*. Are we now to belittle *unum* and glorify *pluribus?*" asks Arthur Schlesinger, Jr.[3] While cultural and ethnic fragmentation is indeed a critical issue facing our society, such an alarmist voice often assumes that underrepresented racial and ethnic groups in America are devoid of creative possibilities and that the taming of the "cults" is the only alternative to the rage of outright chaos and nihilism. By so assuming, those who sound the warning also approach inter-cultural and interethnic alienation as vexatious components in an otherwise comfortable and stable life. Even if the patterns of that vexatiousness are destructive, agonizing, and wrenching to the whole society, the alarmists assume it can be dealt with without fundamental change to the system itself. They believe that no basic change in the patterns of human interrelationships are needed to cope with the alienating state of today's society. This is the fundamental fallacy of the ways the matters of race, ethnicity, and culture are often treated in this society.

Issues of intercultural and interethnic relationships in to-day's society represent a radical departure from prior historically developed notions of human interactions and relationships. These issues call for a basic reconsideration and reconstitution of the ways people in this society historically have related with one another—the domination and subjugation of various groups of people by hegemonic power groups. Reflecting on the Los Angeles event in the spring of 1992, the National Council of Churches Korean delegation proclaimed: "A pillar of flame in L.A. was the melting furnace of black Americans and Koreans. It was the pain of inoculation of two different histories. Our com-mon task is to build a society where a community of different cultures and histories may live together and cooperate with each other. We believe that this should begin with people who have discovered their suffering 'neighbors,' not with government and powerful people."[4] A meeting of "suffering neighbors" in Los Angeles became an occasion for community building across alienated racial and ethnic lines.

This statement gives a glimpse into a radically different way of relating with each other in an age of increased cultural and ethnic consciousness and polarization. "The pillar of flame" that becomes an occasion for the "melting furnace" among estranged groups of people is a new paradigm challenging the euphoric utterance of J. Hector St. John de Crévecoeur during the Ameri-can Revolution: "What then is the American, this new man, who acts upon new principles. . . . Here individuals of all nations are melted into a new race of men."[5] The cultural capital for this society cannot be a melting pot of assimilation. The "melting furnace" is predicated by the honest acknowledgment of painful brokenness and alienation among various groups of people. "Only when we experienced the shock of what happened in L.A. were we able to feel closer to their history of suffering and identify it with the Korean history of suffering." The "melting furnace" is not a melting pot of assimilation, an inclusion of the fringe people into a mainstream. It is a furnace that generates its energy from the deep pain of the experiences of alienation and diversity, the energy that drives the estranged and disparate into a community and therefore into a reconciled relationship. It speaks of a new paradigm, a new societal order unlike the assumed assimilation of *e pluribus unum*.

This new paradigm is formed from a profound tragic sense of life. Much of European American Protestantism has been a success culture, rich in optimism. But many Asian Americans were denied reasons for optimism—if not for hope—throughout most of American history. We know the evil in the human heart by looking at the tragic history of immigrant parents, internment experiences, and experiences of persistent racism and what it has done to us. Many Asian Americans could take the measure of the cramping boundaries of existence—and still affirm. This is the basis of the new paradigm.

Idolatry: The Absolutizing of Prior Historical Developments

Though many do not yet realize it, the heart of the issues of racial and ethnic diversity in the United States is theological in character. Matters of race, culture, and ethnicity in this society are fundamentally the theological concerns of idols and of the One who confronts them with the claim of ultimacy. The escalating alienation among diverse groups in our society stems from the absolutizing of prior historical developments, which sets a societal norm. This invites the idolatry of a particular cultural and racial/ethnic perspective. A challenge to idolatry is a theological challenge. It is a challenge to uncover the depth of the claim of the existing structure of ultimacy. Making up this structure are the hidden rules or anonymous principles that determine the formation and ongoing function of society, language, and subjectivity in cultures.

An idol is an entity of power and control. It is also structural in character. An idol is embedded in the societal and cultural practices, the everyday habits, the linguistic structures, the ways people are raised as racial and ethnic persons. The depth structure of idols refers to the organization of social life in which people of color must represent inferior linguistic, cultural, and social terms, and in which they are formed to think of themselves in negative cultural images.

H. Richard Niebuhr in *The Responsible Self* talks about the shaping influence of the power of our heritage upon life of the present. "Though we choose in freedom, we are not independent, for we exercise our freedom in the midst of values and powers we have not chosen but by which we are bound," Niebuhr observes.[6] In analyzing the depth structure of idols, it is necessary to acknowledge Niebuhr's insistence on the power of our heritage. Sydney E. Ahlstrom locates this power in the Puritan and evangelical traditions.[7] He points out that while the Puritan tradition shaped the religious values in the American revolutionary tradition of democratic government, the Bill of Rights, a free economic order, and the security of property, it also reinforced certain disastrous features of national culture, particularly rampant individualism and racism. "In the complicated root system that nourishes American social evils, two roots are of manifestly special significance. One of them is endemic in the human race—and we call it racism. It destroys our sense of community by keeping human beings and human groups irrationally and obsessively at odds with one another. The other is . . . rampant anarchic economic individualism (RAEI) which destroys our sense of community by keeping human beings in a perpetual state of competition and instability."[8] What is needed is "serious and thorough ideological reconstruction," and it should begin with the critical reassessment of the U.S. religious tradition, which has been elevated to an idol-like status. Without that recovery and reevaluation, Americans will suffer a deepening sense of fatalism, and drift, willy-nilly, toward an ever greater loss of social coherence. What better places exist than communities of faith to engage in such an "ideological reconstruction"? Ahlstrom's warning of some twenty years ago was prophetic in light of recent events.

Central to the issues of race, culture, and ethnicity in America is, therefore, the question of perspectives and histories. The absolutization of a particular historical past has fostered the current climate of racial and ethnic unrest and distrust, because it deeply informed the very patterns of injustice among various groups of people who are judged according to the norms set by the dominating culture and excluded from the construction of those norms. "The Los Angeles uprisings focused media attention on Korean and Asian Americans, Guatemalans, Salvadorans, Chicanos, Mexicans, and African Americans, who were both victims and victimizers. In California, these groups will shape future patterns of race relations which will in turn affect the nation. Asian Pacific Americans will challenge dominant conceptions of race relations and assimilation," says Michael Omi of Ethnic Studies Department, University of California, Berkeley.[9] Unless historical issues of idols are rectified, the patterns will continually reduplicate themselves, for in the received tradition of the society resides the unfolding assumption that liberty is the gift won by the dominant culture, to be condescendingly bestowed by it on those it welcomes.

It is not easy for Americans to realize that history did not have to happen as it did. History need not continue as it is going. It is not easy for Americans to realize that we could rend the veil so that *all* of God's children could relate to one another equally and freely in love, that indeed there are different ways of being with each other. Recalling her grandfather, the main character of *Obasan* describes him: "When he left his familiar island, he became a stranger, sailing towards an island of strangers. But the sea was his constant companion. He understood its angers, its whisperings, its generosity."[10] If U.S. society is indeed "an island of strangers," how can a community be built where each person's dignity and worth are acknowledged, and each person is able to relate equally with other strangers? This question is all-encompassing. It encompasses the development of new forms of community, places in which persons can confront idolatry, where they can receive support, where they can experiment with new forms of relationships. It also encompasses the development of images and practices of community that address not just changing needs within the society but also form the participants in patterns of openness for mutual relationships rather than, as is too often the case with community formation, in structures of closure to all outside the boundaries of that particular community.

Addressing the relationship between Korean Americans and African Americans in the aftermath of the L.A. incident, a group of Korean American Christians uttered the following words: "There was no way we were able to share in their [African Americans'] suffering. Only when we experienced the shock of what happened in Los Angeles were we able to feel closer to their history of suffering and identify it with the Korean history of suffering. At the same time, we also realize that we had disregarded other peoples's history. Our own historical exclusivity caused us to dismiss the cry of the victimized as only anger."[11] The search for a new and different way of being and relating with each other, a new paradigm for community building, is essentially a journey toward joint discovery of self and others. It is a journey toward reconciliation, mutuality, recognition, and creative interaction, even in the midst of ever present conflict, estrangement, and self-assertion at the expense of others.

Theologically, community building is ultimately a gift of grace that we often receive unexpectedly and in spite of our efforts. Cultural and ethnic diversity in America, particularly in its estranged state among different groups, reinforces this reality of life when it is seen theologically. The economy of American cultures is a complex, overlapping, and disjunctive order. It defies any attempt either to schematize or categorize. Even often-quoted center-periphery models do not do justice to the messy, fluid, and often ambiguous interactions among diverse groups of people. Henry Gates, Jr. observes that "the spatial dichotomies through which our oppositional criticism has defined itself prove increasingly inadequate to a cultural complex of traveling culture. Once more, the world itself has outpaced our academic discourse."[12] The world calls for a new way of being and relating with one another that acknowledge this complex and dynamic reality.

A Glimpse of the Future: Hawaiian Churches

There are signs of hope emerging that we are heading toward a new paradigm of community building. America is in a period in which our conception of racial and ethnic categories is being dramatically transformed. Race and ethnicity are not entirely inherent in natural traits, although physical characteristics certainly have a lot to do with how people categorize members of racial and ethnic groups. Rather, racial and ethnic identities derive their meanings from social and historical circumstances. They can vary over time. They are not so much an entity as a dynamic process, in which specific categories acquire and lose meanings over time. Strangers do not stay the same. They interact in a fluid and dynamic fashion, sometimes oppressing each other, other times liberating. This is to say that the very nature of race and ethnicity contains signs, images, and practices that suggest the possibility of transformation and change in ways people relate with each other. Emancipating reconciliation and transformation of relationships are embedded in the ethnic groupings which are themselves in dynamic process. Liberated ethnicity holds some signs of things to come.

A glimpse of this can be observed in the ways in which some churches in Hawaii have developed. The evolving history of the Community Church of Honolulu, United Church of Christ, for example, points to a sign of the emerging pattern of community building. The church was founded in 1934 by a group of second generation Chinese young people. The local Chinese culture began to emerge out of a gradual adaptation process through an exposure to Hawaiian and European American influences. In 1921 the Chinese Department of the Hawaiian Evangelical Association, the predecessor of the present Hawaiian Conference of the United Church of Christ, reported the "pressing need for an English-speaking church for Americans of Chinese ancestry." This was one of the first signs of the emerging Chinese American culture in Hawaii. Ethnicity was the primary consideration for the formation of the church.

The report stressed that neither the Chinese-speaking churches nor the Anglo-Saxon churches could offer a church life to which the young Chinese Americans would respond. "Great need exists for a place of worship with ideals of life and social privileges and form of worship that will establish these new citizens upon Christian, American foundation."[13] Thus the new congregation was formed. The move away from the familiar linguistic and cultural atmosphere of the immigrant parents was by no means easy for the founders of the Community Church. The formation of the church coincided with the gradual emergence of the Chinese American ethnic consciousness.

The church went through several decisive epochs in its history. By the 1970s, however, the Community Church was experiencing gradual but perceptible changes. While the founding Chinese American members and their extended families continued to play key roles in church life, out-marriage (cross-racial and ethnic marriage) and a more flexible social climate in Hawaii had caused a proportional decrease of Chinese American members in the congregation. At the same time, during the 1970s and 1980s, other ethnic groups such as Japanese Americans, Korean Americans, and European Americans began to join the congregation. A temporary dearth of youth membership began to reverse its trend.

In 1986 a European American was called as the director of Christian education. She also worked with the Marshallese ministry. The youth population increased fourfold, from twenty-five to one hundred. Early in its history the church decided not to use the Chinese language in its worship services: English became the sole language of worship. But eventually the Hawaiian language was also blended into the Sunday morning services, particularly through the Gloria, the Prayer of Jesus, and responses, as well as in the occasional singing of Hawaiian hymns. "We took a chance," said founding leader Hung Wai Ching, "Give everybody the freedom to express themselves, and the freedom to listen to a new interpretation. But everybody's got to respect each other and be more broad-minded. And see if we can work together."[14] Is this an expression of *ohana*, Hawaii's cultural expression of the spirit of mutual relationship from which strength and meaning of life are discovered? Or is it a sign of the evolving Chinese American ethnicity in Hawaii? Either way a glimpse of a new model for community building in an ethnically and culturally diverse society is emerging in the Community Church of Honolulu.

Such a model, however, is not formed without the pain of pluralism and the cost of discipleship. The "freedom to listen to a new interpretation" is forged out of a delicate, often confusing and conflicting negotiation among different understandings of community and ethnic identity. Teruo Kawawa, interim pastor of the Community Church and a highly influential former Conference Minister of the UCC Hawaii Conference, noted that the racially and ethnically representational nature of Hawaiian congregations like the Community Church of Honolulu is the fruit of a long and difficult path of racial and ethnic interaction. The transformation has given the congregation a conscious awareness of the centrality of faith in forming a community among often disparate and discordant groups of people. The confessional character of community building meant an acknowledgment on the part of the church members of their own deep-seated prejudice and distrust across ethnic, generational, and class lines. Only when their divisions were confessed in light of faith did the church become open to a new way of relating with each other, a new way of community building. "We had quite a struggle," reflected James Doo, a charter member and six-time council president. But a multicultural and multiethnic community that respects each person's dignity and identity, yet still coheres together, is gradually emerging. The struggle within this community of faith perhaps provides a glimpse of the things to come for all of us.

Community building out of the struggle over interethnic tensions was the issue at the 171st *Aha Pae'aina*, the annual gathering of the Hawaii Conference of the United Church of Christ in 1993. The issue evolved around the apology of the United Church of Christ to the native Hawaiians, *na Kanakamaoli*, for the complicity of the church in the overthrow of the monarchy in 1893. Earlier the General Synod of the UCC in 1991 passed resolution for the apology and directed UCC President Paul Sherry to come to Hawaii for the expression of apology. Now the question is whether the UCC Hawaii Conference should also apologize to *na Kanakamaoli* for the role played by its predecessor, the Hawaiian Evangelical Association, in the overthrow. The churches that are largely clustered around various ethnic groups, many of them Asian Americans, were divided over the proposal for apology.

The Board of Directors, the planning committee of the gathering *aha*, decided to treat the issue within a consensus model of deliberation. Following the presentation of proposals, participants were divided into small groups for Bible study, prayer, and hymn singing. Barriers to community were examined during the session. Emotions ran high, and cultural and formational differences among the participants surfaced in the way the issue of the apology was understood. Then the formal motions were read in silence. People responded, occasionally writing down the underlying problems these formal motions raised. A group then listened and reflected in silence. Then the spokespersons met for consensus on problems felt by the group. Directives were given, and the spokespersons returned with them to their groups. This process was repeated until it was felt by the leaders that there was a basis for consensus.

It was a long and arduous process. The pain of diversity was apparent. But pain was accompanied by promise. Jean Kauffmann, the chair of the Board, reflected on the experience: "It was clear that the body wanted something and was struggling. It was clear that we were in the wilderness. . . . One of the Hawaiian pastors stood and asked the Hawaiian people to stand as he addressed the body. They did. While they were seated throughout the sanctuary, the grouping of many of them formed a ring around the assembly. We were in their midst and being defined by them."[15] The consensus was eventually reached. "We are a microcosm of where the church needs to be, building in the critique with its ethic of risk rather than control and the suffering that is built into the human condition," says Jean Kauffmann. "As the group filed out after a standing ovation and after the noon meal's blessing, the Hawaiian community stayed. One minister spoke to the people about his feeling, and then another shared what was on his heart. After some discussion, they sang a hymn, prayed and went to the dining hall where, before they ate, sang the hymn as an expression of thanks and receiving of the apology and the will of the consensus motion to the rest of the body. Not too many eyes were dry."[16]

These stories remind us once again that the matter of race and ethnicity is appropriately theological in character. This is so because the intertwining actuality of interracial and interethnic alienation in America today and the vision of transformed and reconciled justice in the dynamic reformulating process of ethnicity are the concerns of the gospel. What Christians strive for in faith is the coming Reign of God in which liberation of all shall be the bond that unites us all. The unique composite of disparate diversity of people today becomes the occasion for reconciled diversity of all God's people tomorrow. The common humanity described in the gospel can be understood in depth as it has been transmitted to us in our own specific cultural, social, and spiritual matrix. Therefore, self-identification of each racial and ethnic group is necessary, for the task of self-identification is a precondition to acknowledge the very nature of the gospel. When Elizabeth Tay, a graduate of Pacific School of Religion in Berkeley and now pastor of a United Methodist congregation, says "I encountered God in my ethnicity," it is not a mere separatist statement. We need to construct ourselves in order to be liberated from the oppressive power of the idolatrous national heritage and to participate mutually in community building. It is unrealistic to think that we can now disavow our social, cultural, and ethnic identities; there is not another one to take its place. "My identity as an Asian American woman who has been marginalized in American culture shapes, propels and is analogous to my understanding of God."[17] Such an identity evolves over time from a culturally specific ethnic identity to a more permeable sense of ethnicity. Nevertheless, self-identification is a condition for agency, for social change, liberation. It is an acknowledgment of the historical individuality, historical *conditioning*, of the liberating power of the gospel. Ernst Troeltsch's dictum speaks powerfully to this issue: "The decisive point is above all the individuality of historical forms and the objectivity aspired to in the entire investigation, to measure each form above all only in its particular will and content."[18] Any struggle with ultimacy risks the claim for its encompassing and universal note.

But this note needs to be sounded in a way that does not destroy one's self-identification by engulfing the person in the torrents of an abstract concept of "humanity in general." It is with her own ethnic self-identification that Tay and other Asian American Christians ponder these things—it is with Asian American resources as well as the Christian tradition in its received form that we come to our own understandings of humanity. The question we pose is this: Can the historical individualities that are the great ethnic identities in North America meet in an open conversation about an ultimate liberation in which all people share?

A gospel that transcends all histories is stated in terms of each particular history. To say this is to affirm the integrity and equal worth of the bearers of the presence of the Eternal One in our midst. This is the sense in which theology must try what has not been tried. This is the sense in which our present discussion of Asian American churches only prepares the way for a collective effort, a stride toward the coming Reign of God in which a different way of being with one another—namely, the liberation and justice of each person—becomes the uniting bond for all. Theologically, community building is an engagement in a conversation that is free, free to discover what we did not know ahead of time, free to devise the ordering of our agenda, free to move beyond what we thought would be the marks of the integrity of our inquiry. Community building is proleptic in character. Reconciliation and transformation are imminent but nascent and unpredictable, riding on the power of liberation of silent and invisible groups of people. In the meantime, we will each—in our own cultural and ethnic groupings and together—cultivate a posture of openness toward the reception of the gift of grace, even if the gift comes in a moment to be glimpsed rather than in an accomplishment to be had.

Historical Individuality and Phenomenology of Posturing

The decisive issue forced into the open by Asian American Christians' attempt to express faith through our own cultural and ethnic context is the issue of interpretation of North American history. Speaking of the Asian American churches in the United Methodist tradition, Filipino American Artemio R. Guillermo observes:

> If there is one word that would best describe the development of our Asian American United Methodist churches, it would be "struggle." In my view the word summarizes the birthing, dramatic lives, and triumph against all odds of these fledgling churches in an often hostile environment. Like their ancient brethren, the Israelites, Asian Americans wandered in this vast land of opportunity on an uncertain faith journey. . . . for Asian Americans had to fight their way through, not with swords but with voices, often discordant until their pleas for identity were heard. For it is this innate desire for identity in the midst of diversity in the household of faith that propelled their struggle to get to the Promised Land.[19]

In the midst of the struggle for justice and fair representation, Christian faith embodied and expressed in Asian American churches has transformed Christian identity from a glib and innocuous ecclesiastical affiliation into an intense phenomenology of positioning—a positioning that requires all of one's heart, soul, and mind. Asian American churches' faith-living comes to us in the form of six fundamental questions: Do we have a Christianity which requires us to position against the personal and institutional sin of racism? What do we stand for? Do we take seriously the biblical injunction to do justice, love mercy, and walk humbly with God? With whom do we cooperate? Is our Christian witness in solidarity with those who suffer existential anguish, cultural degradation, political repression, and class exploitation? Upon what do we stand? Is our Christian practice grounded on a solid rock of existential anchorage, particularly of our life in faith community, or does it rest on the sinking sand of epistemological foundationalism? Faith as phenomenology of posturing in society takes seriously the racial, ethnic, and cultural particularities of Asian American churches. Our cultural particularities are important ingredients of faith not only because Asian American Christians protest against the absolutizing and norm-claiming influence of "North Atlantic theology." But it hopefully leads to a decisively new crystallization of insights into the multiethnic and multicultural effort to discern and to serve that liberating vision which all humanity seeks.

Perhaps the decisive question here is not so much whether these new insights elicit a response from the dominant forces within American Christianity in such a way that their insights are transmuted from informants of oppression into contributions toward a shared, liberating future. Though such a question may be crucial, the reality is that Asian American churches are forging ahead, regardless of the tenacious parochialism of the norm setters, with our own phenomenological expressions of faith amidst the rising tide of pluralism in society. Our yearning is for the liberation of the full mosaic that is humanity, not just for the liberation of Asian Americans. Out of our own grappling with matters of faith and ethnicity, our own liminal existence, and experiences of racism, we have come to a significant realization: An America that still refuses to embrace the unique composite that is centuries old but has yet to be celebrated will contain all in the same practiced hostility that means the death of each. In our communities of faith we have come to know, sometimes intuitively but more often than not through our experiential angst, that the variety and diversity of the historical, racial/ ethnic, and cultural components comprising American society are relatable, reconcilable, and perhaps transformable, and that, wherever this is pursued, no matter how infrequent it may be, salutary results have been enjoyed by all involved. Moreover, we learn from the painful history of Asian Americans that a spirit of grace, as experienced both liturgically and in relationships within the community of faith, succeeds in bridging the deep chasm created by the asymmetrical nature of interrelationships and the distrust it creates. What is at stake is an implicit trust in the wisdom of faith community. This phenomenology of posturing is the Asian American Christians' expression of faith.

Ethnic Identity and Reciprocal Creativity

"Imagine, my dear friend, if you can," wrote Alexis de Tocqueville to a friend in France, "a society formed of all the nations of the world . . . people having different languages, beliefs, opinions: in a word, a society without roots, without memories, without prejudices, without routines, without common ideas, without a national character, yet a hundred times happier than our own."[20] The following words of Roy Sano betray the euphemism of Tocqueville a century and a half later: "The melting pot is not a real account of the experiences of racial minorities in the United States. . . . A two-category system is operating at many crucial points in our lives, with the vast majority of colorful peoples assigned to a separate lower category."[21] The question we pose is, once again, Can the historical particularities that are the dynamic ethnic identities meet in an open conversation about an ultimate liberation in which all share? Theology in the context of ethnic pluralism is dependent upon sensitivity to the fact that the components of this pluralism relate to each other in varying degrees; this sensitivity is the precondition of the continuum of reciprocal creativity; and reciprocal creativity is the facilitator of spiritual freedom. This is a freedom expressed in love, a freedom to hear the yearning hope of such a voice as that of Joy Kogawa, and to hear the voices of those who would understand the gospel anew for the sake of mutuality, reconciled diversity, and community building among the estranged.

What this means is that theology is less interested in the order of Christian truth than in Christian life. Its focus is the order of the intended creation as an eventful process that stretches across the whole horizon of Christian existence. Its axial theme is grace, which makes it Christocentric and yet also pneumatological. This is so because the Holy Spirit is the Giver of Grace as well as the Giver of Life. The work of the Holy Spirit signifies the divine initiative in Christian existence and therefore is inseparably related to the way in which people relate to each other even in the midst of estrangement.

From the perspective of those who are on the fringe of society, and particularly for Asian American Christians, this means that grace needs to be understood in relation to a discourse on racial, ethnic, and cultural idolatry, in relation to the contemporary situation. This includes the appropriation of the prevailing systems of thought and popular cultural images. Rearticulation and reformulation of the racial, ethnic, and cultural idols are, in a sense, a desperate necessity in the hegemonic climate in the United States.

What is needed is to name the reality of imposed suffering and destruction which stems from the idolatrous cultural practices that go on in society, particularly from the angle of racial and ethnic diversity. The task is to describe the unjust mind-sets and societal forces that are in need of correction and to analyze basic idolatrous forms of life in need of radical transformation. Such an attempt is perhaps itself an envisioning act of the promised humanity that speaks to a culture caught in the throes of idolatry of the false gods of race, ethnicity, and forms of sovereignty that seem to lead toward self-disintegration.

If Christ is the signal of the promised humanity that Christians affirm, racism represents a profound failure of human imagination. The affirmation of the in-breaking of the grace-filled promise that is reconciled diversity begins with an act of naming the idolatrous forces. Such an act reveals critically and analytically the deprivation and disorder of the hegemonic culture. It opens up the interlocking structures of injustice and alienation among people and identifies possible modes of transformation. If grace empowers us to see and speak of sin, grace also allows us not only to be justified and freed from the gripping power of idols, but also to be transformed into the new life of promised humanity. What is called for is the tenacity to hold onto such a vision of faith, even amid what is the seemingly overwhelming power of the sin of racism. We also need to be as wise as a serpent, politically and strategically astute, to examine critically the actual effectiveness of every step we take, in order to enact the peace of the dove.

The Liberating Power of the Silenced Voices

A society is fundamentally a communion of subjects rather than a collection of perceived objects. Its existence is derived from and sustained by this intimacy of each being with every other being of the society. A society functions as a living organism. There is a unity of the society's functioning that perhaps justifies the use of the term *organic* to describe the inner coherence and integral functioning of the society. A society is so integrated in the unity of its functioning that every aspect of the society is affected by what happens to any of its component members. It cannot survive in fragments. Justice does not come from the barrel of a gun but out of the conscience of a contrite heart. Human diversity is ultimately not some curse, not some problem to be solved, but rather the supreme expression of the creative spirit that undergirds the whole of humanity. The society we have made simply will not survive without the recognition of the interrelated web of humanity in diversity. We need to think of this society as a careful listening of different voices—even if it is an opportunity for listening that some of us were not able to join until recently. The challenge facing America in the next century will be the shaping of a truly mutual and reciprocal interrelation-ship among its member groups, particularly one responsive to the long-silenced cultures of color, each culture conditioned by a different perception of the world. This challenge particularly applies to the dominant and dominating cultures, encrusted with the habits of centuries, who have completely forgotten their own particular ethnic and cultural character.

The promise of society is that this dominance can be broken. The control of the American society by a particular group needs to be shattered in order for their distinct contribu-tions to be made. In the process of moving toward a society of mutuality, Americans whose ethnic roots are in Europe have the opportunity to become what they really are, one human group among many that comprise the mosaic, all of which is in the image of God. To become themselves in the context of this attempt is precisely analogous to the self-determination of Asian Americans and other people of color in the context of this at-tempt. What is taking shape is a future whose reality we can only dimly perceive now, but which we can anticipate with joy, since it will be comprised of all the components of the mosaic. Libera-tion for European Americans is precisely analogous to liberation for *all* people. For them it means becoming not the epitome of humanity in general, but one component in the full mosaic.

While such thinking may still be alien in this society, this is what Asian American Christian leaders have been saying. In the words of the late Baptist minister and prophet Jitsuo Morikawa:

> *We Asian Americans have been made particularly sensitive to the need of theological illumination of public policy and prac-tice, because our lives and welfare have been severely affected by political and economic actions taken by nations of the Pa-cific Basin, whether through wars, colonialism, trade em-bargo, immigration restrictions, trade wars, denials of land ownership, employment restrictions or evacuations. Part of our need for theological answers is appeal to moral norms, in a world where norms are evaded and values are determined by those in dominant power. One part of us fear we live in a*

lawless world where the strong seek to determine our destiny
and the weak desperately need a supreme court of appeal.
Another side of us live with a sense of hope for the future,
what kind of world we seek to create, no comparable vision of
Augustine's "City of God" for the twenty-first century.[22]

This society stands at the threshold of a new era, one that could either tear apart the whole fabric of society with racial and ethnic tension or one that could push us into an affirmation of the basic form of humanity—to relate to one another with justice, mutuality, representation, and love. This is an intractable world cowering before the awesome possibilities of total destruction. Here in North America it seems that we have despaired of our potential to recover, to regroup, and to get on with the humanizing of our sick and decadent social order. Asian American churches exist in a society divided by the excesses of extraordinary racial and ethnic privilege on the one hand and the persistent challenge of racial and ethnic conventions on the other. Anxieties are high. The prospect of despair is to many far less traumatic than the prospects of change. What it means to be Americas is no longer clear, and who should have that privilege will soon become a question of national debate.

In such a time as this, Asian American churches and their leaders speak softly the truth: "Give everybody the freedom to express themselves, and the freedom to listen to a new interpretation. But everybody's got to respect each other and be more broad-minded. And see if we can work together." And yet, this and other voices are not readily heard, not easily acknowledged in society. This land has been blessed by the firm commitment to the high ideals of a nation under God, and cursed in turn for a refusal to honor that commitment. A historic occasion to relent, to repent, and to accept redemption, has been granted. At the very birth of the nation, we had the chance to rid ourselves of the pestilence of slavery by excluding that most barbarous abomination from the new nation, but we failed, despite our determination to adhere to the high principles of human equality, with liberty and justice for all. When this nation fought for democracy, we violated the very principle for which millions of lives were lost, by the internment of our own citizens behind the barbed wire of concentration camps.

The choice ought to have been to use that occasion to restore our own moral integrity by restoring the freedom and dignity of the captives we held. But the nation chose a meaner path, and the insistent rhetoric about liberty and freedom and justice—like the commitment to nationhood under God—rang hollow against the pitiful cries of those whose freedom never reached the agenda of serious deliberation except to be judged as less than human. Since the Civil War and the many wars that followed, and as recently as the Persian Gulf War, we were offered occasions for self-critique and reflection on our quest for justice. But again we balked. The wars were fought. The slaves were freed. Fascist nations were defeated. But the mind-set and the national heritage that made racism and oppression persistent remained intact.

As we watched on television South Central Los Angeles flare up in anger and desperation, and the fragile coexistence among people of different cultural, racial, and ethnic backgrounds burn to the ground, we have once again come to realize that we have not yet developed the fortitude to address seriously the convictions on which this society is so tenuously underpinned. We swab at the symptoms of our ailment, but we have yet to address the disease with the conviction it takes to cure it. In such a time as this, society cannot simply afford to ignore the voice of the silent and silenced Asian American churches. Sang Hyun Lee of Princeton Seminary relates an incident he encountered while traveling in the Rocky Mountains: "[M]y family and I stopped at a Chinese restaurant on a terribly isolated spot in a valley. The owner who greeted and also bid us Goodbye was an elderly Asian man, probably an early Chinese immigrant, who operated that restaurant in that lonely place for many years. I especially remember his aged but intense eyes. In his eyes there was a whole world of untold stories. As we left him, his eyes seem to say, 'Will my stories ever be told to anyone?'"[23] Silence has long pervaded the whole Asian American community, even though recent statistics indicate that we are the fastest growing ethnic population in the U.S. Countless untold stories of wisdom and insights are buried deep beneath the glitter of the life of the powerful. Will our voices ever be heard, taken seriously?

"Silent Mother, you do not speak or write. You do not reach through the night to enter morning, but remain in the voiceless-ness . . . Martyr Mother, you pilot your powerful voicelessness over the ocean and across the mountain, straight as a missile to our hut on the edge of a sugar-beet field. You wish to protect us with lies, but the camouflage does not hide your cries . . . Young Mother at Nagasaki, am I not also there?"[24]

Notes

Introduction

1. Here I rely on George Lindbeck's notion that "[r]eligions are . . . comprehensive interpretive schemes, usually embodied in myths or narratives and heavily ritualized, which structure human experience and understanding of self and world. . . . Stated more technically, a religion can be viewed as a kind of cultural and/or linguistic framework or medium that shapes the entirety of life and thought" (George Lindbeck, *The Nature of Doctrine* [Philadelphia: Westminster Press, 1984], 32–33). What I propose is the view that religion is really a complex web of beliefs, rituals, and practices, rather than a response to some universal human experience.

2. This definition of practice has historical, moral, and epistemological as well as theological dimensions. It counters the conventional separation of practice from theory. Perhaps one of the clearest formulations of practice is that of Alasdair MacIntyre, who defines it as

> *any coherent and complex form of socially established cooperative human activity through which goods internal to that form of activity are realized in the course of trying to achieve those standards of excellence which are appropriate to, and partially definitive of, that form of activity, with the result that human powers to achieve excellence, and human conceptions of the ends and goods involved, are systematically extended.* (After Virtue [Notre Dame, Ind.: Notre Dame University Press], 175)

3. Clifford Geertz, "Thick Description: Toward an Interpretive Theory of Culture" in *The Interpretation of Cultures* (New York: Basic Books, 1973), 10.

4. E. H. Schein, *Organizational Culture and Leadership* (San Francisco: Jossey-Bass, 1985).

5. The framework for this analysis is borrowed from the work of Victor Turner, who described the distinction between "structure" and "communitas" (V. W. Turner, *The Ritual Process, Structure and Anti-Structure* [Chicago: Aldine, 1969; Ithaca, N.Y.: Cornell Paperbacks, 1977]). Structural groups are pragmatic, goal-oriented, and intentionally organizational. Communitas, by contrast, signifies spontaneous relationships of intimate bonds without regard to status, wealth, or property. This is akin to Ernst Troeltsch's distinction between "church" and "sect."

6. Ronald Takaki, *Strangers from a Different Shore: A History of Asian Americans* (New York: Penguin Books, 1989).

7. I rely to an extent on James Hopewell's work *Congregation: Stories and Structures*, ed. Barbara Wheeler (Philadelphia: Fortress Press, 1987), for this dimension of my research.

8. Stanley Inouye, Arlene Inouye, and Sharon U. Fong, "Selected Data from the 1982 Survey of Primarily Japanese Churches in Los Angeles and Orange Counties." Survey summary prepared by Iwa, Inc. (Monrovia, Calif., 1983), 3.

9. Kenneth Uyeda-Fong, *Insights for Growing Asian-American Ministries* (Rosemead, Calif.: EverGrowing Publications, 1990), 133.

10. Takaki, *Strangers*, 13.

Chapter One: Christian Faith and Asian American Ethnicity

1. John G. Ha of Northbrook, Illinois, a sophomore at Dartmouth College, quoted in *Chicago Tribune*, 29 April 1992.

2. Martin E. Marty, *Religion and Republic: The American Circumstance* (Boston: Beacon Press, 1987), 231.

3. C. Eric Lincoln and Lawrence H. Mamiya, *The Black Church in the African American Experience* (Durham, N.C., and London: Duke University Press, 1990),

4. Roy I. Sano, "One-Third U.S. Immigrants Are Pacific and Asian Americans," *JSAC Grapevine* 10, no. 9 (April 1979).

5. Maxine Hong Kingston, in Marilyn Yalom, ed., *Women Writers of the West Coast* (Santa Barbara, Calif.: Capra Press, 1983), 16.

6. "Chinese on Kauai," *The Friend*, 1 May 1879, 44.

7. William Mamoru Shinto, "The Role of Religion in Asian American Communities," unpublished paper, 7 December 1975, 4.

8. Ibid.

9. Andre Siegfried, quoted in H. Richard Niebuhr, *The Kingdom of God in America* (New York: Harper and Row, 1935), 17.

10. John Jay, quoted in Michael Walzer, "Pluralism in Political Perspective," *The Politics of Ethnicity* (Cambridge, Mass.: The Belknap Press of Harvard University Press, 1982), 2.

11. Andre Siegfried, *America Comes of Age: A French Analysis* (New York: Harcourt, Brace and Company, 1927), 34, 35.

12. Ibid., 35.

13. *Debates and Proceedings in the Congress of the United States, 1789–1791* (Washington, D.C.: U.S. Congress, 1834): vol. 1, pp. 998, 1284; vol. 2, pp. 1148–56, 1162, 2264.

14. Philip Park, "Asian Christians and the Bicentennial," in *Bicentennial Broadside* (New York: National Council of Churches, 1976), 27.

15. Alfred T. Mahan, *The Problem of Asia and Its Effect upon International Policies* (Boston: Little, Brown, 1900) quoted in Ronald Takaki, *Iron Cages: Race and Culture in 19th-Century America* (Seattle: University of Washington Press, 1979), 269.

16. Sydney Ahlstrom, in Roger van Allen, ed., *American Religious Values and the Future of America* (Philadelphia: Fortress Press, 1978), 13.

17. William Speer, *The Oldest and the Newest Empire: Chinese and the United States* (Pittsburgh: R. S. Davis and Company, 1870), quoted in *Proceedings of the Sixth Triennial Meeting of the National Conference of Christian Work Among the Chinese in America*, 21–27 June 1971, 34.

18. Ibid., 35.

19. Gilbert Lum (at Second National Conference of Christian Work Among the Chinese in America, 17–19 September 1958).

20. Jose Movido, "Co-Existence as a Strategy for Ethnic Empowerment in the American Church" (Doctor of Ministry diss., Claremont School of Theology, 1976).

21. Artemio R. Guillermo, ed., *Churches Aflame: Asian Americans and United Methodism* (Nashville: Abingdon Press, 1991), 99.

22. Centennial Celebration Coordinating Council, *"A Centennial Legacy": History of the Japanese Christian Missions in North America*, vol. 1 (Japanese Christian Churches of America, 1977), 37.

23. Ibid.

24. Ibid.

25. Richard Drinnon, *Keeper of the Concentration Camps: Dillon S. Myer and American Racism* (Berkeley: University of California Press, 1987).

26. Ibid., xxvii.

27. Ibid., 31.

28. Ruth Sasaki, quoted in Jorge Ribeiro, "Fashioned out of Silence," in *Intersect* (October 1992): 29.

29. Daisuke Kitagawa, *Issei and Nisei: The Internment Years* (New York: Seabury Press, 1967).

30. Shingu Shimada, *A Stone Cried Out* (Valley Forge. Pa.: Judson Press, 1986), 132.

31. Nisei Christian Oral History Project, *Nisei Christian Journey: Its Promise and Fulfillment*, vol. II (Nisei Christian Oral History Project: 1991), 130–31.

32. Lester E. Suzuki, "The Role of the Church During the Evacuation Experience," in *Hono-o* (winter 1992): 4.

33. Nobu Miyoshi, *Identity Crisis of the Sansei and the Concentration Camp* (Alameda, Calif.: Sansei Legacy Project, 1992), 33.

34. Andrew Lind, *Hawaii's Japanese: An Experiment in Democracy* (Princeton, N.J.: Princeton University Press, 1946), 101–62, quoted in Takaki, *Strangers from a Different Shore*, 402.

35. Nobu Miyoshi, *Identity Crisis*, 33.

36. Rudolph J. Vecoli, "Ethnicity: A Neglected Dimension of American History," in Herbert J. Bass, *The State of American History* (Chicago: Quadrangle, 1970), 70ff.

37. Michael Yoshii, "Japanese American Bazaar Tradition and Racial Ethnic Identity," presented at Programme for Theology and Culture in Asia, 10 July 1992, 14.

38. Yoshiko Uchida, *Desert Exile* (Seattle: University of Washington Press, 1982), 42.

39. Diane Mei Lin Mark, *Seasons of Light: The History of Chinese Christian Churches in Hawaii* (Honolulu: Chinese Christian Association of Hawaii, 1989), 299.

40. Eui-Young Yu, "Korean Communities in America: Past, Present, and Future," *Amerasia Journal* 10, no. 2 (1983): 3.

41. Ibid., 40.

42. Ibid.

43. Takaki, *Strangers from a Different Shore*, 472f.

44. Ibid., 488

45. Sharon Thornton, from her sermon "Don't Enryo!" preached on 4 October 1992 at Christ Church of Chicago, UCC.

46. Nellie Wong, "Day of the Dead," in *Dreams in Harrison Railroad Park: Poems* (Berkeley, Calif.: Kelsey Street Press, 1977), 120.

47. Roy Sano, "Response to Dr. Chung Hyun-Kyun's Presentation," Seventh World Council of Churches Assembly, Canberra, Australia, February 1991, 4–5.

48. Robert N. Bellah, et al., *Habits of the Heart: Individualism and Commitment in American Life* (Berkeley: University of California Press, 1985), 223.

49. Ibid., 8.

50. "Priority Concerns of Pacific and Asian American United Methodists," *e/sa* (Engage/Social Action—Publication of the Board of Church and Society of the United Methodist Church), vol. 11, no. 4 (April 1983): 10.

51. Harry H. L. Kitano and Roger Daniels, *Asian Americans: Emerging Minorities* (Englewood Cliffs, N.J.: Prentice-Hall, 1988), 105.

52. Jonah Chang, in Artemio R. Guillermo, ed., *Churches Aflame: Asian Americans and United Methodism* (Nashville: Abingdon Press, 1991), 135.

53. Ibid., 152.

54. Takaki, *Strangers*, 485.

55. Wesley Woo, "Worship: Celebrating God's Redemptive Acts in Human History," in *Pacific and Asian Americans: Emerging Models for Ministry*, proceedings from the Working Conference on Emerging Models for Ministry, Pacific School of Religion, Berkeley, Calif., 22–23 May 1988 (Berkeley, Calif.: Pacific and Asian American Center for Theology and Strategies), 22.

56. Alexis Canillo and Joan May Cordova, *Voices: A Filipino American Oral History* (Stockton: Filipino Oral History Project, Inc., 1984), 29.

57. Michael Yoshii, "Bazaar Tradition," 18.

58. Kingston, in Marilyn Yalom, ed., *Women Writers*, 16.

59. Chang, in Artemio R. Guillermo, *Churches Aflame*, 140.

60. "The Story of the first Fifty Years at the Community Church of Honolulu: 1934–1984," prepared by the Fiftieth Anniversary Committee of the Community Church of Honolulu, 1984, p. 5.

61. Hung Wai Ching, quoted in Diane Mei Lin Mark, *Seasons of Light*, 294.

62. *Remembering: The Sojourners in Asian-American History* E19.

63. Kitano and Daniels, *Asian Americans: Emerging Minorities*, 176f.

64. Ron Tanaka, *Koreatown Weekly*, 8 September 1980, 2.

65. Kitano and Daniels, 191.

66. Wesley Woo, "A Socio-Historical Starting Point for a Pacific and Asian American Theology," unpublished paper delivered at Pacific and Asian American Theological Conference (23–25 January 1987).

67. Wesley Woo, "Asians in America: Challenges Posed for the Presbyterian Church, U.S.A.," 13.

68. Jean Bethke Elshtain, "Citizenship and Armed Civic Virtue: Some Critical Questions on the Commitment to Public Life," in *Community in America: The Challenge of Habits of the Heart*, eds. Charles Reynolds and Ralph V. Norman (Berkeley: University of California Press, 1988), 53.

69. Wesley Woo, "Worship," 23.

Chapter Two: Holy Insecurity—Asian American Faith Quest for Indentity

1. William M. Shinto, "Alternative Futures for Asian American Christians," unpublished paper, March 1975, 308.

2. William Greenbaum, "America in Search of a New Ideal: An Essay on the Rise of Pluralism," *Harvard Educational Review* 44, no. 3 (August 1974): 419.

3. Rita Nakashima Brock, "Dusting the Bible on the Floor: The Loss of Innocence and the Power of Wisdom in Asian American Women's Writing," *In God's Image* 11, no. 3 (1992): 9.

4. Arnold Park, a twenty-one-year-old Korean American political science major at Northwestern University, quoted in *Chicago Tribune*, 29 April 1992, 6.

5. Arthur M. Schlesinger, Jr., *The Disuniting of America: Reflections on a Multicultural Society*, The Larger Agenda Series (Knoxville, Tenn.: Whittle Direct Books, 1991), 2.

6. Louis Agassiz, quoted in Arnold Krupat, *Ethnocriticism: Ethnography, History, Literature* (Berkeley: University of California Press, 1992), 233.

7. Ronald Takaki, *Strangers from a Different Shore: A History of Asian Americans* (New York: Penguin Books, 1989), 328, 101.

8. Audrey Lorde, *Sister Outsider: Essays and Speeches* (Trumansburg, N.Y.: The Crossing Press, 1984), 115.

9. Ibid., 115–16.

10. Eileen Sunada Sarasohn, ed., *The Issei Portrait of a Pioneer: A Japanese Oral History* (Palo Alto, Calif.: Pacific Books, 1983), 275.

11. Elaine H. Kim, *Asian American Literature* (Philadelphia: Temple University Press, 1982), 102.

12. Marya Castillano Sharer, quoted in Fred Cordova, *Filipinos: Forgotten Asian Americans* (Seattle: Demonstration Project for Asian Americans, 1983), 165.

13. Nelson Nagai, *The Other Side of Infamy* (Church, Calif.: Association of Asian American Educators, 1983).

14. Maureen Lai-Ping Mark, "Understanding Asian American Racial Identity: An Asian American Woman's Perspective on Why Asians Shouldn't Be Viewed as 'White,'" *Integrity* (a publication of Chicago Clergy and Laity Concerned), vol. 1, no. 5 (March–May 1993).

15. Asian American Student Alliance, *Unity of Three* (Santa Cruz, Calif.: UCSC Asian American Student Alliance, 1977), 133.

16. Joseph Kitagawa, *The Christian Tradition: Beyond Its European Captivity* (Philadephia: Trinity Press International, 1992), 110–11.

17. *The Inter Ethnic Theological Colloquies* (7–10 Nov. 1985), seminar held at San Francisco Theological Seminary, San Anselmo, Calif.

18. Bok-Lim C. Kim, quoted in Stanley Sue and James K. Morishima, *The Mental Health of Asian Americans* (San Francisco: Jossey-Bass, 1982), 122–124.

19. Kathryn Choy-Wong, "Parable of the Peoples: A Story About the Spirit's Movement in Asian American History," *In God's Image* 11, no. 3 (1992), 34.

20. *Remembering: The Sojourners in Asian-American History* (San Francisco: Asian-American Christian Education Curriculum Project, Golden Gate Mission Area, Synod of the Pacific, Presbyterian Church USA, 1979), 37.

21. Sang Hyun Lee, "Liberating Pilgrimage to Home: An Asian American Theology" (unpublished draft), 6.

22. Beverly W. Harrison and Carter Heyward, "Pain and Pleasure: Avoiding the Confusions of Christian Tradition in Feminist Theory," in Joanne Carlson Brown and Carole R. Bohn, eds., *Christianity, Patriarchy, and Abuse: A Feminist Critique* (New York: The Pilgrim Press, 1989), 165.

23. Eui-Young Yu, "Occupation and Work Patterns of Korean Immigrants in Los Angeles," in Eui-Young Yu, Earl M. Phillips, and Eun Sik Yang, eds., *Koreans in Los Angeles: Prospects and Promises* (Los Angeles: Koryo Research Institute/Center for Korean American and Korean Studies, California State University, 1982), 90.

24. Bok-Lim Kim, *Korean American Child at School and at Home* (Washington, D.C.: U.S. Government Printing Office, 1980).

25. See Kil-Nam Roh, "Issues of Korean American Journalism," in *Amerasia* 10, no. 2 (1983): 89–102.

26. Harry H. L. Kitano and Roger Daniels, *Asian Americans: Emerging Minorities* (Englewood Cliffs, N.J.: Prentice-Hall, 1988), 114.

27. Elaine T. Matsushita, "Asians Weighing Costs of Blending into U.S. Culture," *Chicago Tribune*, 29 April 1992, 6.

28. K. Samuel Lee, "KA Churches Must Reforcalize [sic]; Reaching Youth Top Priority," *KoreAm Journal*, June 1991.

29. Ibid.

30. Charles Ryu, "Koreans and Church," in Joann Faung Jean Lee, *Asian Americans* (New York: The New Press, 1991), 162.

31. *Hokubei Mainichi* (Japanese American newspaper, published weekly in Los Angeles), 21 July 1992.

32. Ibid.

33. Ibid.

34. Ibid.

35. Michi Weglyn, *Years of Infamy: The Untold Story of America's Concentration Camps* (New York: William Morrow, 1976), 21.

36. Ibid.

37. Ibid.

38. Joseph M. Kitagawa, *The Christian Tradition: Beyond Its European Captivity* (Philadelphia: Trinity Press International, 1992), 102.

39. Robert Lifton, *Death in Life: Survivors of Hiroshima* (New York: Vintage Books, 1969), 94.

40. Robert Lifton, *The Broken Connection: On Death and the Continuity of Life* (New York: Simon and Schuster, 1979), 169.

41. Lifton, *Death in Life*, 253.

42. Florence Date Smith, "Days of Infamy," in *Messenger* (Church of the Brethren publication), November 1988, 12.

43. *Hokubei Mainichi*, 6 August 1992.

44. Sumio Kuga, ed., *A Centennial Legacy: History of the Japanese Christian Missions in North America* (Chicago: Nobart, 1977), 31.

45. Soomee Kim Hwang, "In-Between Colors Have Names, Too," in PAACE: *Pacific and Asian American Christian Education*, newsletter 7, no. 1 (March 1992): 5.

46. Fran Toy, "Cutting Through the Double Bind," *Pacific People* (Occasional Newsletter of the Pacific and Asian American Center for Theology and Strategies, Berkeley, Calif., New Year, 1990), 5.

47. Ibid.

48. Elaine Kim, "Patriarchy and Asian American Community," an unpublished paper presented at the Pacific and Asian American Conference on Theology and Ministries, Berkeley, California, 1986, 8.

49. Ibid., 1.

50. "Patriarchy and Women Within Pacific/Asian American Communities," a discussion following Elaine Kim's presentation at the Pacific and Asian American Conference on Theology and Ministries, 1986, in *Branches* (Pacific and Asian American Journal of Theology and Ministry), vol. 3, no. 1 (summer 1987): 34.

51. Ibid., 35.

52. Elaine H. Kim, *Asian American Literature: An Introduction to the Writings and Their Social Context* (Philadelphia: Temple University Press, 1982), 250.

53. Kim, "Patriarchy and Asian American Community," 7.

54. Diana Akiyama, "It's Time to Take Stock," in *Branches*, Pacific and Asian American Journal of Theology and Ministry (fall/winter 1990): 13.

55. Kim, "Patriarchy and Asian American Community," 13.

56. *Hokubei Mainichi*, 6 August 1992.

57. Soomee Kim Hwang, "In-Between Colors."

58. Rita Nakashima Brock, "Dusting the Bible on the Floor: The Loss of Innocence and the Power of Wisdom in Asian American Women's Writing," *In God's Image* 11, no. 3 (1992): 3f.

59. Ibid., 10.

60. Sang Hyun Lee, "Liberating Pilgrimage to Home," 17.

61. The quote comes from an interview in Christ Church of Chicago, U.C.C.

62. Wesley Woo, *Sojourners in Asian-American and Biblical History*, Adult Series (San Francisco: Asian American Christian Education Curriculum Project, Golden Gate Mission Area, Synod of the Pacific, Presbyterian Church USA, March 1979), 38.

63. Wontae Chu, "Immigration Theology," in Joann Faung Jean

Lee, *Asian Americans: Oral Histories of First to Fourth Generation Americans from China, the Phillippines, Japan, India, the Pacific Islands, Vietnam, and Cambodia* (New York: New Press, 1992), 171.

64. Jitsuo Morikawa, "95th Anniversary Address: Japanese-American Churches in the U.S.A." (unpublished sermon).

65. Ibid.

66. Ibid.

67. From the Centennial Worship Celebration, Japanese Christian Mission in North America, 9 October 1977. Quoted in Wesley Woo, *Sojourners*.

68. Kim, "Patriarchy and the Asian American Community," 12.

69. Morikawa, "95th Anniversary Address."

Chapter Three: A Stone That Cries Out

1. Marilyn Yalom, ed., *Women Writers of the West Coast* (Santa Barbara, Calif.: Capra Press, 1983), 16.

2. For a helpful discussion on this matter, see Patricia Hill Collins, *Black Feminist Thought: Knowledge, Consciousness and the Politics of Empowerment* (New York: Routledge, 1991).

3. Joseph Kitagawa, *The Christian Tradition: Beyond Its European Captivity* (Philadelphia: Trinity Press International, 1992), 98–99.

4. Robert N. Bellah et al., *Habits of the Heart: Individualism and Commitment in American Life* (Berkeley: University of California Press, 1985), 148.

5. Ibid., 152.

6. William Greenbaum, "America in Search of a New Ideal: An Essay on the Rise of Pluralism," *Harvard Educational Review* 44, no. 3 (August 1974): 414.

7. David M. Schneider and Raymond T. Smith, *Class Differences and Sex Roles in American Kinship and Family Structure* (Englewood Cliffs, N.J.: Prentice-Hall, 1973), 20.

8. Bellah et al., *Habits of the Heart*, 151–52.

9. Frank Y. Ichishita, "Asian American Racial Justice Perspectives," in *Church and Society* 72, no. 4, 28.

10. Wesley Woo, "Asians in America: Challenges Posed for the Presbyterian Church (U.S.A.)," an unpublished paper, 28 February 1987, 7.

11. Calvin Chinn, "Toward a New Missiology: From a Chinese-American Perspective," *Branches* (fall/winter 1990): 15.

12. Wesley Woo, "Asian Americans, Culture, Justice, and the Reformed Tradition" (unpublished paper), 4.

13. Wesley Woo, *Sojourners in Asian-American and Biblical History*, Adult Series (San Francisco: Asian-American Christian Education Curriculum Project, Golden Gate Mission Area, Synod of the Pacific, Presbyterian Church USA, March 1979), E19.

14. Jeff Murakami, "Pacific and Asian American Theologies Within the Socio-historical Context of the Current Crises in the Pacific Basin," *Branches* 3, no. 1, errata.

15. Ichishita, "Asian American Racial Justice," 30.

16. Nicholas Iyoya, "Asian American Churches and Social Involvement," in *Church and Society* 64, no. 3, p. 47.

17. The comment was made at the gathering of Midwest Regional Meeting of Asian American United Methodists (November 1992 at St. John's United Methodist Church, Oak Park, Illinois).

18. Maureen Lai-Ping Mark, "Understanding Asian American Racial Identity: An Asian American Woman's Perspective on Why Asians Shouldn't Be Viewed as White," *Integrity* 1, no. 5 (March–May 1993).

19. Iyoya, "Asian American Churches," 46.

20. Ibid.

21. Ibid., 47.

22. Ira Lee, "The Past, Present and Future of the Presbyterian Church U.S.A. Among the Chinese" (paper presented at the Second Meeting of the Asian Presbyterian Caucus, Pacific Palisades, Calif., 27 April 1963), 5.

23. Amadeo Zarza, "Emergence of the Filipino Presbyterian Church" (paper presented at the Second Meeting of the Asian Presbyterian Caucus, Palisades, Calif., 27 April 1963).

24. Brian Kenji Ogawa, "Japanese American Churches and the Asian Movement" (paper presented at the Second Meeting of the Asian Presbyterian Caucus, Palisades, Calif., 27 April 1963), 30.

25. "Challenge to the Churches—Toward a Racially Just World" (report of the International Consultation on Racism and Racial Justice, convened by U.S. Commissioners of the Programme to Combat Racism, 17–21 January 1988), 3–4.

26. Ibid., 10.

27. Douglas John Hall, *Lighten Our Darkness: Toward an Indigenous Theology of the Cross* (Philadelphia: Westminster Press, 1976).

28. David Y. Hirano, "Shame and Racism" (paper presented at the UCC Consultation on Racism, 2 May 1989), 6.

29. Ibid., 7.

30. Wesley Woo in "Worship: Celebrating God's Redemptive Acts in Human History," in *Proceedings from the Working Conference on Emerging Models for Ministry* (Berkeley, Calif.: Pacific and Asian American Center for Theology and Strategies, 22–23 May 1980), 23.

31. Ibid., 24.

32. Roy I. Sano, "A Theology of Struggle from an Asian American Perspective," *Branches* (fall/winter 1990): 11.

33. *Remembering: The Sojourners in Asian-American History* (San Francisco: Asian-American Christian Education Curriculum Project, Golden Gate Mission Area, Synod of the Pacific, Presbyterian Church U.S.A., March 1979), 9.

34. Ibid.

35. Karl Barth, *Church Dogmatics*, vol. III, part 2 (Edinburgh: T. and T. Clark, 1960), 265.

36. Benjamin Reist, *Theology in Red, White, and Black* (Philadelphia: Westminster Press, 1975), 70.

37. Sano, "A Theology of Struggle," 11.

38. Maureen Lai-Ping Mark, *Integrity* 1, no. 5 (March–May 1993).

39. Eui-Young Yu, "We Saw Our Dreams Burn for No Reason," *In God's Image* 11, no. 3 (1992): 32.

40. Sano, "A Theology of Struggle," 9.

41. James H. Cone, *A Black Theology of Liberation* (Philadelphia: J. B. Lippincott Company, 1970), 80.

42. Ruth Ocera Cortez, "Theology of Struggle: Some Notes and Reflections," *Branches* (fall/winter, 1990), 6.

43. Nobuko Joanne Miyamoto, "What Are You?" *Amerasia* 1, no. 3 (1971). Used by permission.

44. Sano, "A Theology of Struggle," 11.

45. Carlos Bulosan, "Letter in Exile," *Amerasia* 13, no. 1 (1986–87): 133.

46. Wesley Woo, "Asians in America," 16.

47. Stephen Steinberg, *The Ethnic Myth: Race, Ethnicity, and Class in America* (Boston: Beacon Press, 1989), 262.

48. James Baldwin, *The Fire Next Time* (New York: The Dial Press, 1963), 117–18.

49. H. Richard Niebuhr, *The Social Sources of Denominationalism* (New York: H. Holt and Company, 1929), 30.

50. Frederick Buechner, "The Pontifex," in *Hungering Dark* (New York: Seabury Press, 1968), 47.

51. Edward Shils, "The Culture of the Indian Intellectual," *The Sewanee Review* (April and June 1959): 45–46.

52. William Greenbaum, "America in Search of a New Ideal: An Essay on the Rise of Pluralism," *Harvard Educational Review* 44, no. 3 (August 1974): 414.

53. Paul Nagano's statement is taken from the course "Ministry in a Multi-Ethnic/Cultural Society" at Pacific School of Religion, spring 1987.

54. Rita Nakashima Brock, "Dusting the Bible on the Floor: The Loss of Innocence and the Power of Wisdom in Asian American Women's Writing," *In God's Image* 11, no. 3 (1992): 10.

55. Bulosan, "Letter in Exile," 133.

56. Brock, "Dusting the Bible," 3.

57. Lalrinawme Ralte, "Asian and Asian American Women in Theology and Ministry," *In God's Image* 11, no. 3 (1992): 39.

58. Ibid.

59. From the Centennial Worship Celebration, Japanese Christian Mission in North America, 9 October 1977.

60. Ibid.

Chapter Four: Conclusion

1. Joy Kogawa, *Obasan* (Boston: David R. Godine, 1981).

2. Henry Louis Gates, Jr., *Loose Canons: Notes on the Culture Wars* (New York: Oxford University Press, 1992), xii.

3. Arthur M. Schlesinger, Jr., *The Disuniting of America: Reflections on a Multicultural Society* (CITY: The Larger Agenda Series, Whittle Direct Books, 1991), 2.

4. "An Ecumenical Visit to L.A. and the Position of the Korean Church," *Branches and Pacific People* (fall/winter 1992–93): 9.

5. Letter III in Hector St. John Crevecoeur, *Letters from an American Farmer* (New York: Dutton, 1957).

6. H. Richard Niebuhr, *The Responsible Self* (New York: Harper and Row, 1963), 44.

7. Sydney E. Ahlstrom, in *American Religious Values and the Future of America*, ed. Rodger van Allen (Philadelphia: Fortress, 1978).

8. Ibid., 21.

9. Michael Omi, quoted in *Policy Issues to the Year 2020: The State of Asian Pacific America—A Public Policy Report* (Los Angeles: The LEAP Asian Pacific American Public Policy Institute and the UCLA Asian American Studies Center, 1993), 7.

10. Kogawa, *Obasan*, 18.

11. "An Ecumenical Visit to L.A.," 9.

12. Gates, *Loose Canons*, 191.

13. Report of the Chinese Department to the Hawaiian Evangelical Association Board (Hawaiian Mission Children's Society, 1921).

14. Hung Wai Ching, quoted in Diane Mei Lin Mark, *Seasons of Light: The History of Chinese Christian Churches in Hawaii* (Honolulu: Chinese Christian Association of Hawaii, 1989), 294.

15. From an unpublished document by Jean Kauffmann on the 171st *Aha Pae'aina*.

16. Ibid.

17. Elizabeth Tay, "I Encountered God in My Ethnicity," *In God's Image* ll, no. 3 (1992): 13.

18. Ernst Troeltsch, *Der Historismus und seine Ueberwindung*, quoted in Benjamin A. Reist, *Toward a Theology of Involvement: The Thought of Ernst Troeltsch* (Philadelphia: The Westminster, 1966), 65.

19. Artemio R. Guillermo, ed., *Church Aflame: Asian Americans and United Methodism* (Nashville: Abingdon Press, 1991), 12.

20. Alexis de Tocqueville, *Selected Letters on Politics and Society*, ed. Roger Toesche (Berkeley: University of California Press, 1985), 38.

21. Roy I. Sano, "Beyond the Melting Pot: A Two-Category System," in *From Every Nation Without Number* (Nashville: Abingdon Press, 1982), 37.

22. Jitsuo Morikawa, "Pacific and Asian American Theologies Within the Socio-historical Context of the Current Crises in the Pacific Basin," *Branches* 3, no. 1 (1987), 14–15.

23. Sang Hyun Lee, "Liberating Pilgrimage to Home: An Asian American Theology" (unpublished draft), 187.

24. Kogawa, *Obasan*, 242.

Bibliography

"An Ecumenical Visit to L.A. and the Position of the Korean Church." *Branches and Pacific People* (fall/winter 1992–93): 9.

Bellah, Robert N., et al. *Habits of the Heart: Individualism and Commitment in American Life.* Berkeley: University of California Press, 1985.

Brock, Rita Nakashima. "Dusting the Bible on the Floor: The Loss of Innocence and the Power of Wisdom in Asian American Women's Writing." *In God's Image* 11, no. 3 (1992): 9.

Chinn, Calvin. "Toward a New Missiology: From a Chinese-American Perspective." *Branches* (fall/winter 1990): 15.

Drinnon, Richard. *Keeper of the Concentration Camps: Dillon S. Myer and American Racism.* Berkeley: University of California Press, 1987.

Greenbaum, William. "America in Search of a New Ideal: An Essay on the Rise of Pluralism." *Harvard Educational Review* 44, no. 3 (August 1974): 419.

Guillermo, Artemio R., ed. *Churches Aflame: Asian Americans and United Methodism.* Nashville: Abingdon Press, 1991.

Hokubei Mainichi (Japanese American newspaper, published weekly in Los Angeles), 21 July 1992.

Ichishita, Frank Y. "Asian American Racial Justice Perspectives." *Church and Society* 72, no. 4, p. 28.

Iyoya, Nicholas. "Asian American Churches and Social Involvement." *Church and Society* 64, no. 3, p. 47.

Kim, Elaine. "Patriarchy and Asian American Community" (unpublished paper presented at the Pacific and Asian American Conference on Theology and Ministries, Berkeley, Calif., 1986).

―――. *Asian American Literature*. Philadelphia: Temple University Press, 1982.

Kitagawa, Daisuke. *Issei and Nisei: The Internment Years*. Seabury Press, 1967.

Kitagawa, Joseph M. *The Christian Tradition: Beyond Its European Captivity*. Philadelphia: Trinity Press International, 1992.

Kitano, Harry H. L., and Roger Daniels. *Asian Americans: Emerging Minorities*. Englewood Cliffs, N.J.: Prentice-Hall, 1988.

Kogawa, Joy. *Obasan*. Boston: David R. Godine, 1981.

Lifton, Robert. *Death in Life: Survivors of Hiroshima*. New York: Vintage Books, 1969.

Mark, Diane Mei Lin. *Seasons of Light: The History of Chinese Christian Churches in Hawaii*. Honolulu: Chinese Christian Association of Hawaii, 1989.

Miyoshi, Nobu. *Identity Crisis of the Sansei and the Concentration Camp*. Alameda, Calif.: Sansei Legacy Project, 1992.

Morikawa, Jitsuo. "95th Anniversary Address: Japanese-American Churches in the U.S.A." (unpublished sermon).

Niebuhr, H. Richard. *The Kingdom of God in America*. New York: Harper and Row, 1935.

Sano, Roy I. "A Theology of Struggle from an Asian American Perspective." *Branches* (fall/winter 1990): 11.

Schein, E. H. *Organizational Culture and Leadership*. San Francisco: Jossey-Bass, 1985.

Schlesinger, Arthur M., Jr. *The Disuniting of America: Reflections on a Multicultural Society*. Knoxville, Tenn.: The Larger Agenda Series, Whittle Direct Books, 1991.

Shinto, William Mamoru. "The Role of Religion in Asian American Communities." Unpublished paper, 7 December 1975.

Takaki, Ronald. *Strangers from a Different Shore: A History of Asian Americans*. Penguin Books, 1989.

Toy, Fran. "Cutting Through the Double Bind." *Pacific People* (newsletter of the Pacific and Asian American Center for Theology and Strategies, Berkeley, Calif., New Year, 1990).

Uyeda-Fong, Kenneth. *Insights for Growing Asian-American Ministries*. Rosemead, Calif.: EverGrowing Publications, 1990.

Weglyn, Michi. *Years of Infamy: The Untold Story of America's Concentration Camps.* New York: William Morrow, 1976.

Woo, Wesley. "Asians in America: Challenges Posed for the Presbyterian Church (U.S.A.)." Unpublished paper, 28 February 1987.

———. "Worship: Celebrating God's Redemptive Acts in Human History." In *Pacific and Asian Americans: Emerging Models for Ministry.* Proceedings of the Working Conference on Emerging Models for Ministry, Pacific School of Religion, Berkeley, Calif., 22–23 May 1980.

———. *Sojourners in Asian-American and Biblical History* (Adult Series). San Francisco: Asian-American Christian Education Curriculum Project, Golden Gate Mission Area, Synod of the Pacific, Presbyterian Church USA, March 1979.

Yalom, Marilyn, ed. *Women Writers of the West Coast.* Santa Barbara, Calif.: Capra Press, 1983.

Yu, Eui-Young. "Occupation and Work Patterns of Korean Immigrants in Los Angeles." In Eui-Young Yu, Earl M. Phillips, and Eun Sik Yang, *Koreans in Los Angeles: Prospects and Promises.*

———. "We Saw Our Dreams Burn for No Reason." *In God's Image* 11, no. 3 (1992): 32.

Index